'People are trapped in history and history is trapped in them.' – James A. Baldwin

Contents

Foreword 2
Introduction 5
- Where is Bangladesh? 5
- Where is Sylhet? 6
- Where is Westminster? 6
- What did we hope to find? 6
- What we found 8

Methodology 15
- The research and editorial team 15
- Sample 15
- Transcripts and translating 16
- How we conducted our research 17
- How we analysed and presented our findings 18

* * *

Chapter 1: Motivations for moving to London 19
Chapter 2: Hopes and fears 24
- Their own hopes 24
- Their hopes for their children 26
- Their fears for their children 27
- Their own fears 31

Chapter 3: Day-to-day life 34
- The living arrangements 36
- Occupation 42
- Adjusting to Britain 47
- Difficulties during the 1960s & 1970s 50

Chapter 4: Languages 59
- Barriers 60
- Opportunity 63

Chapter 5: Home away from home 67
- Keeping it Halal 67
- Clothes 71
- The community 73
- Helping one another 78

Chapter 6: Views of some non-Bengalis 82
Chapter 7: Support services in Westminster 86
- School 87
- Local people and services 90

Chapter 8: Leisure time 107
- With friends 107
- With family 110

Chapter 9: Women's stories 111
- Role at home 112
- Integrating into society 113
- Employment 116

Chapter 10: Religion 120
- Religious practice 121

Chapter 11: Relationship with children 127
- The teaching of religion 129
- Education 130

Chapter 12: Preserving Bangladeshi culture 131
Chapter 13: The melting pot 136
- Relationships with local people 137
- Getting involved in local issues 138
- Having mixed friends 139
- Mixed marriages 140

Chapter 14: Life in Westminster at present 144
Chapter 15: The British / Bangladeshi 149
Chapter 16: Future hopes 155
Chapter 17: Bangladeshis in the eyes of others 157
Chapter 18: Views of our community researchers 160
Chapter 19: The first generation 173

Foreword

Abdul Aziz Toki
Project Director

Following the success of "The Legacy of Women's Contributions" in 1971, Central London Youth Development (CLYD) launched its second oral history project. We encouraged our young researchers and volunteers to gather information about their community from various public sources.

During a visit to the Westminster Archive Library, our team was disappointed to find that there were very few resources available. There were no substantial records of the history of immigration or the role Bangladeshi immigrants played in introducing cultural, social, and economic diversity.

A significant number of Bengalis settled in Westminster between the 1960s and 1970s. Sharing their stories is the focus of our project. Despite the challenges of moving to a foreign land, they persevered. Today, the British Bangladeshi community is thriving.

Uncovering the Stories

The hopes, fears, ambitions, and perceptions of life of our elder generation were not documented, so we had to explore them first. This could not have been done without help from our local communities, welfare clubs, politicians, and individuals who can make a difference. Young members of our organization took it upon themselves to explore the lifestyles of our parents and grandparents when they migrated to the UK.

We would like to thank the Heritage Lottery Fund, especially the grant officers, for their substantial contributions to this project. Uncovering these wonderful stories was a team effort, and we are grateful to the following people who supported our cause:

- Ms Karen Buck, Member of Parliament for North Westminster (Labour Party)
- Mr Ansar Ahmed Ullah, Director, Swadhinata Trust
- Mr Andrew Mederick, Director, Fourth Feathers Youth Club
- Mr Rory Lalwan, Senior Archives and Local Studies, Westminster Archives Library
- Mr Simon Ryder, Chief Executive, Beauchamp Lodge Settlement

We are extremely proud and thankful for everyone's contributions and support, including those not mentioned here.

Bringing the Stories to Our Youth

Our participants found collecting oral histories of British Bangladeshis in Westminster challenging but worthwhile. The project encouraged them to explore their dual identity as British and Bangladeshi, and what it means to be second or third-generation immigrants. This process proved valuable in encouraging people from these generations to interact with their elders and learn from their experiences. Participants were interviewed in both English and Bengali to ensure the authenticity of their stories.

Additionally, we interviewed individuals who interacted with the first generation of Bengalis, providing a holistic perspective of their struggles and courage. We now have enough authentic information to share their stories.

Celebrating Life and Our Culture

"Faces of Westminster" is a community-led piece of research documenting the experiences of people who moved to the UK 50 years ago, offering firsthand perspectives of their settlement. Although this is just a small sample, this book sheds light on significant aspects of migration and how life as a Bengali Muslim and Asian in the UK has evolved over the past few decades.

Today, Bengalis, like any other ethnicity, face their share of issues. However, we also have many reasons to celebrate our history, culture, heritage, and legacy. We are very proud and grateful to our young people for gathering and preserving these stories before they were lost forever. We hope that future generations are inspired to follow in their footsteps and create unique platforms for these stories to be shared.

Introduction

Where is Bangladesh?

Once a key part of British India, Bangladesh is now a sovereign state in South Asia, located at the tip of the Bay of Bengal. The country is known for its rich cultural and ethnic diversity, and shares borders with India and Myanmar. Bengali, which is the national language of the country, is also spoken widely in neighbouring states in India.

Bangladesh is home to 166.2 million inhabitants, making it the eighth largest country in the world in terms of population, and the fifth largest in Asia. The country has a fast growing economy and is one of the major industrial and technology outsourcing service providers in the world.

Where is Sylhet?

Sylhet, the 'spiritual capital of Bangladesh', lies along the banks of the Surma River in the north-eastern region of Bangladesh. The city is known for its tropical climate, rain forests, tea estates, subtropical hills and river valleys, making it one of the top tourist destinations in Bangladesh.

Sylhet is also known as the 'second London', due to the increasing number of Sylheti Bengalis moving to the UK, particularly London, which now has prominent British Bangladeshi communities, including those in Westminster. Sylheti is the regional language and is primarily spoken in the city of Sylhet.

Where is Westminster?

Westminster is a borough in central London, located within the City of Westminster, along the north bank of the River Thames. Westminster is known for its historic landmarks, tourist attractions, and a culturally and ethnically diverse population. 14.52% of the population is Asian British (2011 census), making it the second largest ethnic group in the borough.

Westminster is known as one of the most well-preserved boroughs in London. It is home to several communities of people with Bengali ancestry. The borough now has a growing population of first and second generation British-Bengalis, who make up the second largest Asian-British ethnic group.

What did we hope to find?

The history of Bangladeshi migration to the UK has been of great interest to both academics and community historians, with contributions such as 'Tales of Three Generations of Bengalis in Britain' by the Swadhinata Trust, and Caroline Adams's 'Across Seven Seas and Thirteen Rivers'.

Although publications like this offer a useful foundation for subsequent explorations, Faces in Westminster offers a nuance in the turbulent story of Bangladeshis in the UK, in that it presents a voice of the community from a different part of London.

Previous studies focusing on the migration of Bangladeshis to East London, particularly the Tower Hamlets area, have explored the role of seamen or Lascars, and the prevalence of the docks in the lives and motivations of East End Bengalis. Shifting the geographical focus to Westminster offers an alternative reading of this community history, whereby we learn of the varied motivations for moving to and settling in Westminster, and the distinctions between them and their counterparts settling further East.

The main purpose of our research is to record the memories of Bangladeshi migrants settling in Westminster during the 1970s. We wanted to:

1. Fill the gap in knowledge about first generation Bangladeshi migrants who settled in Westminster

2. Understand the hopes and fears that Bangladeshi people had when settling and raising their families in Westminster

3. Hear female voices and understand how their experiences differed to their male counterparts

4. Understand how Bangladeshi migrants integrated into Westminster life and how they managed cultural differences

What we found

Below is a summary of some of our key findings.

Who came to Westminster and why?

Through 'Faces of Westminster', we have found that Bengali migrants who came to the UK in the 1970s were often economically motivated, especially young single men who made up most of the first arrivals. They were keen to support their families financially and seek educational opportunities abroad. Women often came to join their husbands who had arrived earlier. This challenges the assumptions made by some non-Bangladeshi historians and local people that the 1971 War of Independence in Bangladesh fuelled migration, or that Bengalis were here just to escape poverty.

Our interviewees didn't tend to give this as a direct reason for their decision to migrate. Our opinion from the stories we have collected is that the first generation of Bengali men sought opportunity - they came to the UK looking for an adventure. For the majority of them, returning back to their beautiful country, where the weather was always warm, the food was rich and the people were friendly, was always part of their plan.

Hopes and fears

We found that Bengali parents felt very hopeful about entering the UK. Although making money was a key factor, a number of Bengalis spoke of their distinct desire to educate themselves and their children. At the same time, they were also worried about the impact a British education would have on their new British Bengali children, that these children may 'forget' or even deny their rich Bangladeshi heritage.

When asked about this they often denied any fears, or simply gave brief answers. Although it is possible that they came here with many hopes and aspirations, we also wondered if there were any barriers preventing them from sharing these difficult stories. We found that women were more likely to share their experiences of personal distress than men in the community.

Stories of settling in Westminster

Some of the greatest struggles that Bengali migrants discuss are their living arrangements. Men spoke of the severe overcrowding, to the point that they were renting a bed in a room full of people for a few hours a night. Women often came later, when things were better, and were shielded from the worst of the overcrowding, joining their families when they had begun to settle and were able to make more private arrangements.

When we discussed employment, it appeared that in line with our predictions, the Bangladeshis who settled in Westminster mostly worked within the catering industry. Although it is often assumed that Bangladeshis only worked in Indian restaurants, the stories we uncovered show that they actually worked across a diverse range of cuisines. Another finding from our research was that individuals often started working from a very early age.

Many interviewees spoke of their worries about 'skinheads' and instances of racism and physical violence. Most of the interviewees reported that they were able to integrate well and got along with people of all backgrounds, though some also reported being affected by the tensions rife in that period.

Home away from home
Amongst the tales of hardship, a powerful theme which we identified was how supportive the Bangladeshi community was to one another. The Bangladeshi culture is collectivist, and Bengali migrants brought that with them to London.
    They would openly approach other Bengalis to offer their support and share what little they had. Their stories share themes such as trust, loyalty, respect and care for the community and neighbours - traits we fear are gradually being lost as we become a generation more concerned with our own needs and that of our immediate families. People often spoke about family members and friends who were able to offer them a place to sleep and get on their feet.

The female perspective
Our findings also shed some light on how Bengali women functioned during the 1970s. As their husbands tended to work away, women were often left to run the home. This meant that they were in charge of caring for children and had greater interaction with the communities in which they lived.
    A common misconception is that being a homemaker was a Bengali woman's only role. However, we have stories of women who worked a range of jobs such as sewing, in schools or even in a bakery.

Language
Although it was something of a barrier to integration for the Bengali community, language also helped unite the Bengali diasporas at that time. Language plays such an integral role in Bengali identity, and was the catalyst for the War of 1971 against West Pakistan. It was interesting to trace the role of language when Bangladeshis settled in Westminster. People encountered difficulties due to language barriers and we heard tales of the journeys

people had taken in order to learn the English language. Bengali migrants who understood English would often act as ambassadors and advisors within the community, helping others to fill in forms and access the services they needed.

Preserving the Bangladeshi culture
Bengali migrants wanted to preserve important parts of their culture and identities. For many, this most visibly manifests itself in food, clothing, language and religious practice. As second and third generation British Bangladeshis, we have been brought up with Bangladeshi cuisine available at home whenever we wanted it. For us, it has become the norm to have access to the rich foods of Bangladesh. However, this quality cuisine was not as accessible for first generation migrants. In fact, it was this generation's passion for food that established the curry in Britain and made it possible for us to have this beautiful part of our roots so present in our everyday lives.

Unlike Bangladeshi, men who largely adopted British clothing, women were more likely to continue wearing traditional outfits such as the saree or salwar kameez. Just as they have been able to preserve traditional Bangladeshi food, they ensured traditional garments are easily accessible for our generation.

First generation parents also worried that their children would not speak the Bengali language. Many parents encouraged their children to speak Bengali at home and took them on visits to Bangladesh so that they could experience the culture of their motherland and retain the language.

Despite parents' desires to retain Bengali culture, we found this first generation were also accepting of their children adopting parts of British culture, as they wanted them to integrate with the society in which they lived.

Islam
As second / third generation British Bengalis, Islam and religion has always been a prominent part of our identity. Things like prayer and observing Ramadan are woven into our lives and encouraged through friends and family and even on TV. However, a common theme shared by early Bangladeshi migrants was that access to Islam was more limited. As a result, it became rare that people would fast during Ramadan or celebrate during Eid. Islamic principles have strengthened through the generations.

The first Bengali migrants were settling in a new country where the culture and living standards were very different to their own. As a result, we found stories of great determination regarding the difficulties of nurturing children between two very different cultures.

These parents showed great dedication in teaching their children about Bangladeshi culture and the Islamic way of life, whilst also prioritising their children's mainstream educational needs. Given that this generation of parents did not tend to practice Islam as frequently and were not as fluent in English, it was surprising to hear how much value they placed in instilling these values into their children.

A perspective from non- Bangladeshi professionals
Speaking to non-Bengali professionals who worked in Westminster during the 1970s, we found a fondness for the Bengali community as they moved in and brought some of their culture and traditions with them. Local politicians and service providers were keen to help the Bengali community settle. They spoke particularly about integration, how and where it happened, and some of the barriers to it.

We also spoke with the migrants about services or organisations that supported people as they adjusted to Westminster. We found that people often integrated via their children's schools – education was a priority and parents were encouraged to communicate with non-Bangladeshis. Schools tended to be receptive and accommodating to migrants of all backgrounds.

With time, those with little English became more able to live in the developing Bengali community without requiring meaningful interaction with their English neighbours. However, as they became more settled, some became more invested in local concerns. This led to some Bengali representation in the local council.

Stories of integration
Bengali children were mostly allowed to integrate with children of other backgrounds because parents understood that this was a part of their new environment. However, these same parents tended to strongly disapprove of marrying non-Bengalis.

Although cultural differences caused many parents to feel uncomfortable, some did accept the idea that they could not prevent their children from developing strong feelings for non-Bengalis.

Westminster has seen many changes across the years and is generally seen as being well developed with a strong infrastructure and a dense population. However, some families have been priced out and it is now seen as a wealthy area.

The communities have also changed; some Bengalis remain, but the Irish and Afro-Caribbean communities are mostly not around anymore, while a large Arab community has moved in.

Bengalis also have less of a presence in local jobs. However, there is now more diversity in the area and cultural festivals like Eid are celebrated by a wider population. Our interviewees feel some sense of community has been lost nonetheless. Many believe that the new generation treats each other with less respect than before, citing attitudes on buses as a prime example, for instance passengers not giving up their seats for the elderly, or drivers not seeming to care for their passengers.

Where are their children now?

In the present day, these parents express great pride in their children, particularly as they see a young community of practicing Muslims. This is often considered an important marker of success for parents. There is also a general pride in viewing their children as equally Bengali and British.

Parents are especially positive about education and financial security. They speak about how their children have integrated with British life and begun successful careers in the UK. There are, however, fears of what will happen with the next generation, caused by uncertainty about how those children will be raised. The Bengali community longs for future generations to attain prosperity and success, while retaining some of the religious and cultural values of their ancestors.

The Bengali community in the UK is now established and remains close-knit. We wonder, however, if younger generations have lessened communication and travel to Bangladesh, maybe as a result of many of our immediate and extended family living in London. We can see from their stories that the first generation of migrants experienced the UK very differently to us. The Bangladeshi community continues to progress in the UK – education has been strong and the successes are paying off for many in a range of different fields. This is not the case for everybody, however, and many continue to experience a similar quality of life to their parents.

Methodology

The research and editorial team

Our team of young people are all of second or third generation British Bangladeshi heritage. Most of us grew up in Westminster or have a connection to the area. We bring with us a range of skill sets which we have used to explore this important era for British Bangladeshi heritage.

We are a group of volunteers who have sought to share the stories we have collected. We have tried to present our methodology and findings in the clearest form for all readers. We welcome corrections for future work and editions.

Sample

We recruited our sample of participants through the use of word of mouth - a method known as snowball sampling. Those of us who were raised in Westminster contacted our family members and relied on them to nominate other members of the community. This process allowed us to reach as many as possible within this unique population.

This technique means that the stories we have collected will not necessarily be representative. Our participants are predominantly Sylheti speaking (a variation of Bengali) and Muslim. While this group made up the vast majority of this newly arrived community, they cannot speak for all Bangladeshi migrants settling in 1970s Westminster.

More regrettably, we didn't manage to recruit as many women to our research as we would have liked. Nonetheless, we have been able to uncover many incredible stories and hope they can be further explored in the future, particularly with women, non-Sylheti speakers, and non-Muslim Bangladeshis.

We would also like to highlight that none of the stories included in this publication have been verified as factual, through any external resources. We do not take responsibility for any of the claims made by the participants. Our aim was to collect stories from people's own memories. It is expected that discrepancies will occur between people's accounts.

Transcripts and translating

We conducted most of the interviews in Sylheti and then translated and transcribed them into English. This piece of work was conducted by a group of second generation British Bangladeshis.

Although we have tried our best to make sure the interviews have been translated as honestly and transparently as possible, it is likely that some of the true authenticity of each participant's stories will have been lost or even misinterpreted during the translation process.

Each interview lasted approximately 20 minutes and time constraints made it difficult for each interview to be translated by more than one researcher. However, we maintained good communication between ourselves and discussed any stories that any member of the team may have struggled to translate.

Language plays a crucial role in constructing our knowledge of the world. The Sylheti language and dialect is very different to the English language, and we found that Sylhetis will often use the same word to describe a range of concepts.

For example, the Sylheti word 'chinta' can be interpreted in many different ways - 'worrying', 'thinking', or 'being afraid or concerned'. Therefore, each researcher who translated a document naturally understood the Sylheti stories through their own interpretation of the Sylheti and English languages.

We invite readers to read each quote with an open mind and explore alternative perspectives to each story, as this will enable you to appreciate the richness of each person's unique experiences.

How we conducted our research

We began our research process by bringing the team of young people together to discuss and develop the themes we wanted to explore through our interview questions. We then arranged relevant training sessions in order to equip us with some basic skills. We then developed and agreed an interview script based on this.

Following this, we contacted potential interviewees through our networks. We asked for consent to record and translate the interviews and use them in this publication. We used a Dictaphone, a video recorder, a pen and paper, and also held copies of our questionnaires.

We shared the interviews, transcription and editing duties across the team.

How we analysed and presented our findings

The editorial team read through each transcript to collect shared themes. We grouped the themes together and used this structure to create the chapters of the book. Time and resource constraints mean we have largely published the recollections from our interviews as they were told to us, without our own extensive analysis.

We hope that readers will take away a good understanding of the stories and their own perspectives about what they mean. As you will notice, a few of the stories will fall into more than one chapter. During the structuring phase, we discussed these recollections as a team and made decisions about where to place them.

Chapter one

Motivations for moving to London

We found that Bangladeshi migration to the UK in the 1970s was often economically motivated, especially the young single men who made up most of the first arrivals. They were keen to support their families financially and seek educational opportunities abroad.

Women often came to join their husbands who had arrived earlier. It is assumed by some non-Bangladeshi historians that the 1971 War of Independence in Bangladesh fuelled migration.

Our interviewees didn't tend to give this as a direct reason for their decision to migrate. We found instead that they were looking for an adventure and seeking new opportunities.

Mr Abdul Hannan: I came here to join my family and live a nice life. Bengali people who had settled in London would often visit Bangladesh during their holidays. They would spend a lot of money. This motivated me to come to London and be in that same position one day.

Mr Khalil Miah: My dad and uncle were very interested in this country so I thought it would be nice to come here. I thought by coming here I would have a nice life.

Alhaj Md Abdun Noor: In March 1964 my father had enrolled me into the local college in Bangladesh, but when I saw local people moving to London, I took the opportunity as well. My older brother had come earlier than me, and advised me to stay in Bangladesh and continue my study but I didn't listen to him. I came on my own, and then lived with my brother here in Westminster. Initially, coming to London was very exciting, but once I'd arrived it felt very different to what I expected.

My father asked me to stay in Bangladesh and continue with my studies and then get a good job. In fact, he told me that I was only allowed to come to London for five to seven years, after which I would have to return to Bangladesh.

I thought the same: I would be here for a few years, earn some money and then go back. I still keep that same thought in my mind, and wish to return to my country, but what can I do? I did not want to bring my family here, that is why they came much later than me.

I had no intention of staying here, so there was no point bringing my children here. But my family members and relatives put a lot of pressure on me, and convinced me to bring them here.

Mrs Anowara Begum: I came here with my husband. He

left Bangladesh and was very happy so he told everyone to join him. At the time I was 27. When I came here, there were a few Bengalis, I'd meet them on the streets.

Mr Abdul Sobur: I was very happy. I was earning money and was able to go back to my home country. If I had invested in Bangladesh then I would have to be there permanently and leave this country.

Mr Abdul Moobin: In 1963, after my graduation exams, before I'd even received my results, my friends had encouraged me to move to London. At the time I was looking for a job, as my education had come to an end. It was then that a friend told me about the UK. I thought I could have a better life. That is what inspired me.

Alhaj Lala Miah: I was studying in Bangladesh whilst my father was in the UK. One time he came back to Bangladesh and told me that he wanted me to be educated in the UK. That is when we made the decision for me to come. At the time, it was rare for family members to join their families in the UK. First I went to Birmingham, then I moved to South Wales. In 1968 I was 22 years old and moved to Westminster.

Mr Kobir Miah: I came because England was well renowned, it was an educated country and I knew I could improve my life by coming here.

Haji Arob Ali: In 1963 many people came to London, and news was passed on from one person to another. There were very few opportunities for us in our country at that time, so we were always looking for ways to be better off. We heard that the UK offered better employment and more opportunities to earn money.

Mrs Harisun Nessa: I never had plans to live here

permanently, I never even bought utensils or saucepans. My plan was come here with my children and show them a new country and leave. I bought one pan thinking I would leave it behind once I left the country. Really! In terms of me staying long term, once my children began to grow up and settle down, I knew I would never leave and that we would be staying.

Haji Fazar Ali: I started school and then started working. I came to London to make money.

Alhaj Uster Ali: I came to Britain because I have a big family. I was the second eldest of five brothers and three sisters. I came to this country because I believed by coming here I could help my family by putting my siblings through school and also supporting my country. I really thought about it.
   Nobody told me to come here, and I wasn't young when I did. I understood that my life would be better if I came to London or America. I filled in the applications myself to come to this country. I arrived in London in 1963 and settled in Westminster in 1975.

Mrs Hosne Ara Moobin: I came with my husband. At the time I had no children.

Alhaj Abdur Rahman: When I was in Bangladesh, I had a shop and one day I went to town to buy some materials. It was then I noticed a big queue in front of the employment office. I got the address from there and wrote to the British High Commission.
   Within a week, I received a letter to collect my voucher. Before me, only two others from my village had gone to the UK. Luckily, I was able to contact them when I arrived in October 1963.

My family's financial situation was not ideal, I was the only one supporting them. I owned a small business and knew it would not be possible to improve their quality of life through this.

Therefore, moving to London would mean that I could support my family and improve their lives. At the time I was about 22 years old. As my family's financial situation was not good, my priority was to put them first and thus chose not to marry before leaving Bangladesh.

Haji Surok Meah: It was a totally different environment. One of my relatives returned back to Bangladesh, but I had started working so I remained here. My parents and the rest of my relatives were in Bangladesh.

In fact, my parents were well off and they were strongly against me moving to the UK, but as I was desperate to come here, one of my uncles supported me and convinced my parents to allow me to fly to the UK. My father never asked me for any money; instead, he inspired me to become established here.

Mr Joe Hegarty: I know that the war in Bangladesh and independence in 1971 saw waves of people migrating for various reasons, and those most involved wanted to get away for obvious reasons. But there were also economic pressures because Sylhet is a tremendously poor area.

(Editors' note – Bengalis were economic migrants, and were not fleeing war or persecution. And Sylhet is one of the most prosperous regions in Bangladesh.)

Mr Guthrie McKie: To escape from poverty of course – the same reason I left Scotland.

(Editors' note – they were looking for better opportunities).

Chapter two

Hopes and fears

Although the community faced their share of struggles, we found a general positivism in the interview responses, reflecting a cultural desire to focus on achievements rather than talk about struggles.

Their own hopes

Mr Fazal Miah: My hope was to see London, earn money and build a good house for a better life.

Mr Abdul Hannan: I thought that if I came, I would be able to make some money.

Ms Khaleda Qureshi: When I left Bangladesh I had this image of London being a beautiful country that I would enjoy, but when I landed I saw the surrounding areas as dark. All the buildings looked black so my first impression, in fact, was that our country is much nicer than this one.

Haji Arob Ali: I was not very educated, yet I hoped to have a job here and create a better life.

Mr Abdul Moobin: I was excited, as I was going to a new place, a developed country with a high standard of living. I intended to pursue education, stay here for a maximum of five years, finish off my studies and then return home. I never intended to stay here forever. All of my family members were in Bangladesh, and none of my relatives were here, just friends.

Mrs Hosne Ara Moobin: I didn't really have any expectations of the UK. I did have some concerns about what might happen to me in the future. Back home (Bangladesh) I had a good job, I felt confident that I would be able to do something with my life. However, in the UK, I thought that I would have to start my life from scratch.

First I had thought that I would return to Bangladesh in a short period of time. It never occurred to me that I would be spending the rest of my life here. My husband had a good job here; he was a government employee and his future was here. So I started thinking about my future and thought that I should do something as well.

Mr Kobir Miah: Yes, I was very excited, many of my friends told me this was a great country. I thought I would study, get an education and find a good job.

Ms Noorjahan Begum: I wasn't very worried, actually I felt happy. I thought that I could have a better life here, better food and clothes. I was happy because my family was very small. In fact, I was with my children so no family members were left behind in Bangladesh.

Mr Abdul Sobur: It was not bad, it actually felt good. There were opportunities to earn money - I was able to earn good money. During that time, the daily wage for workers was 50p. I would earn around £11 for the whole week. So I worked a lot.

(Editors' note – according to a historic inflation calculator - if we convert £11 from 1970 to the current value in 2016 - Mr Abdul Sobur would earn £163 per week.)

Alhaj Muhib Uddin: I thought if I could come and make at least £20,000, I could go back to Bangladesh and start my own business. With that amount of money, in those days you would be set up for life.

Alhaj Lala Miah: I did not have any expectations. It was my father – he wished to educate me in this country and therefore bought me with him. He sent me to school. I studied for some time, and picked up some of the English language, but not very much. When my father returned to Bangladesh, I started working. Basically, from one restaurant job to another.

Their hopes for their children

> *We found that parents felt very hopeful upon entering the UK. Financial gains were a key factor and a number of Bangladeshi parents spoke of their desire to educate their children.*

Mrs Anowara Begum: I was very excited to be coming, and very happy to eventually join my husband with our children. The children's schooling would be good. I always heard about this country, living standards, education, etc from my husband. He often mentioned the parks, friends, museums and many other things.

Ms Azizun Khatun: My only hope was that my children would be highly educated, and my son has fulfilled my dream. He has bought a house, completed his education and is earning good money.

Alhaj Abdur Rahman: Three of my children were born in Bangladesh. They came here with their mother. I had a dream that my children would get a better education and would have a better quality of life.

Alhaj Muhib Uddin: My main thoughts were to give my children a good education.

Their fears for their children

In line with their hopes, some of the Bangladeshi migrants' greatest fears were about education. Parents also worried about negative influences on their children's behaviour.

Ms Azizun Khatun: I was worried about their education. If they didn't do well, I worried about what they would do in this country. Their education and how they would grow was my main worry. It's why I always took them to the library. Even during the holidays I would mostly be in the library with them.

I always feared that they would become delinquents. In fact, I have seen white people worry about the same thing. I always had feelings that they may drop out of school without any formal education, or be influenced by poorly behaving peers. Secondary school age was really important. This is when they start going to the cinema or even clubs.

Mrs Harisun Nessa: I would never let them stray. Wherever they would go, I would be right behind them. In our country we have a saying about cows and making sure they go in a certain direction (laughs), I did the same with my kids. I wanted the best for my kids.

Mrs Hosne Ara Moobin: Honestly I did not think of anything else except education. I always thought about how we could raise them to have a better education.

Dr Andrew Elder: The different generations reacted to living in London differently. There was the first generation of people who had grown up mainly in Bangladesh, and then their children and their children's children. You could see different attitudes and different conflicts between those three generations.

I would say the most 'free' generation, who seemed to be at ease with being in London, was probably the second generation, because the third generation seemed to become more religious and more restricted. Not all of them but some of them.

It was very interesting to observe the different reactions to being a migrant population settling in a new environment, and how they affected the different generations and the tensions between the generations. Actually, you can't generalise about it because it is different in every family.

I can remember lots of worries in the older generation about the westernisation of their children, and the anxieties that caused and the tensions in families about behaviour patterns that might have seemed quite normal to the second generation who had grown up here.

Sometimes, that second generation became very strict parents of their own children. It's a very complex business and I don't think you can generalise about it but I remember finding it interesting.

Haji Surok Meah: My only fear concerned how they would be educated and become decent human beings in a different culture.

> *When we began our investigation, we had an assumption that Bangladeshi parents would have a number of fears over raising their new British-born children. We predicted that they would discuss the possibility of being rejected by the western culture, or struggling to integrate into society.*

> *However, our findings did not accurately reflect that prediction. In fact, we found that most parents feared one thing in particular - their children would 'forget' or even deny their rich Bangladeshi heritage.*

Ms Khaleda Qureshi: Our greatest fear was that our children would change their identity, that they would adopt the English culture. There were no mosques or places where they could learn about the Bangladeshi culture - how would they keep their religion or their culture?

Haji Arob Ali: I always worried that if they adopted another culture it would be a big problem for us. Of course, they have to live in this country and have to know the culture, but we always told them to respect our culture.

Haji Arob Ali: I always thought about how they would maintain and manage themselves in between two cultures. Whether they would convert to another culture or anything like that.

Mr Abdul Moobin: Raising your children as British - it was a big concern; you don't know what can happen. It was a big worry.

Haji Arob Ali: The children who were born in this country showed very little sympathy for Bangladesh, so I don't hold much hope that the future generations will preserve or maintain their culture and identity. Some of my relatives have never taken their children to Bangladesh, so how will they know their own country, relatives or culture? How will they love their country and culture?

Alhaj Lala Miah: In terms of culture, I felt that my children were following me, following my culture, and following my family. I never thought that by mixing with a different culture, my children would adopt that culture rather than their own.

> *We also noticed a common concern regarding safety.*

Mr Abdul Moobin: Safety was the main concern. That they were able to go to school carefully and return safely. I never faced any racial problems.

Mr Kobir Miah: My biggest fear was that my children would follow the wrong crowd, so I encouraged them to hang around with the right groups of people. I advised them it's very important to practice religion. That was my biggest fear and I still fear it today. It didn't matter if my children had English friends as long as they were good children. It didn't matter what race my children would hang around with, there are great children in every group.

Alhaj Abdur Rahman: I didn't have any fears for my children as they were living with me and were taking my advice. I expected them to be ok, although there have been times when they have disagreed with me. However, I am sure that in the future, they will understand and agree with me.

I had some fears about their safety. When they were going to school, I hoped that they would stay safe on the way there and back. Most parents had the same concerns. I personally did not face any problems. During my first eight or nine years I hardly went out - most of the time I was busy with my work.

Their own fears

From our investigation we found that when Bangladeshi migrants were asked about their fears, they often denied they had any, or gave brief answers. Although it is possible they came here with many hopes and aspirations, we also wondered if there were any barriers preventing them from sharing these difficult stories.

We found that women were more likely to share their emotional experiences than the men.

Alhaj Abdur Rahman: I was always worried about whether or not I will be able to adapt to this weather and environment.

Haji Fazar Ali: I was young and did not understand anything. I was scared of coming to the UK.

Ms Azizun Khatun: It was not exciting for me as I was leaving my family members; I was the eldest in my family so I knew I would miss them. I had no immediate family members from my father's family. I was not scared to be in this country, as I had some confidence that at least I had managed to complete my secondary school education before coming to this country.

I got married after my SSC (GCSEs). My uncle hoped to educate me further but my father arranged this marriage so he was very upset.

Mrs Anowara Begum: At the time I worried about language. How I will speak with people? What would I say if a teacher asks me a question about my children? My English was so limited I only knew how to say 'What is your name? Where are you from?'

Alhaj Uster Ali: No, at that time I wasn't scared because I was real tough. The railway station I used to work in had little to no Bengalis. The few Bengalis who used to work in the railway station used to work in the canteen and those who didn't used to get picked on by the Irish and Jamaicans.

When I first came, they used to try to pick on me, but I showed them and from then on they all called me Ali Baba. I can remember throwing two Irish men on the floor. It wasn't that I liked fighting but it was self-defence, you needed to be able to defend yourself in this country.

New country, different language. Our language is Bengali. Though I studied English, it was not the spoken kind, so I thought it was difficult to adjust to this country. I was a little worried, but not that much as I was confident that at least I knew some English.

Mr Fazal Miah: I did not worry about anything; my faith was in Allah, in this country. How much more can you do?

Mrs Harisun Nessa: I was never scared, even though I left everyone behind. I had even left my eldest daughter behind, my sister in laws took care of her. I could not bring her as I was told that there was a lack of space, I thought about her a lot. She came a few years later, I put in an application through a family friend. Although all the problems started once I arrived here (laughs). My middle son caused me the most stress. The others were OK but he was the worst.

Chapter three

Day-to-day life

Our interviewees told us of a very different Westminster, one which has been subject to constant change ever since they arrived.

Alhaj Md Abdun Noor: There is a big difference in Westminster now. Over time, there has been a lot of development. For example, buildings during that time were not as big or as modern. In fact, when we came to the country, we saw some of the places and houses that had been destroyed during the Second World War. Where Centre Point now is, there was just a big bomb blast hole. It was later on that the big building was built. There were quite a few bomb ruins in Gerrard Street.

Mr Khalil Miah: At that time it was quite difficult, because we were inexperienced and there were not many of us. We didn't have our families and I didn't have my mother. Most of us were around the West End and Aldgate. There were about 20-25 of us who were part of the first generation.

Mrs Harisun Nessa: There weren't any Bengalis here. I didn't really like it. We were alone. There weren't Bengalis, so we didn't have anyone to speak to. I used to go for walks along the streets. I had a pram and child lead; I would take my kids with me for a walk.

I would walk to Paddington and dropped my kids to Nursery school. The other kids would be left at home with my husband who worked night shifts, so he would be sleeping upstairs.

Dr Andrew Elder: In the 1970s the population was much less varied than it is now. There was a West Indian population. There were Jewish migrants who came in before the war and after it, Irish and West Indian people, and what are often called traditional working class English families living around Church Street.

Then the Bengali communities arrived in the 70s, then there was a massive influx of people from other countries later on. It was mixed. Church Street market was different. The big department store was still a department store - it became Alfie's. The Arab immigration hadn't happened yet.

Lisson Green Estate had only just been built. It was quite a problematic area because lots of people were housed from all over London, many who had quite considerable problems or so it seemed to us. It was quite different from now because those flats have been sold and modernised. Some of the more expensive areas - there's a French bank down there now - were not there. It was quite a different area. It was a slightly more homogenous area than it is now.

The living arrangements

Some of the greatest struggles that Bengali migrants discussed were their living arrangements. People spoke about severe overcrowding - to the point that men were renting a bed in a room full of people for a few hours a night. Women often came when things were better and were thus shielded from the worst of this.

Amongst the tales of hardship, we also noticed tales of support and kindness. People often spoke about family members and friends who were able to offer them a place to sleep and get on their feet. Community support is a very dominant trait of the Bangladeshi community - something that becomes clearer in later chapters.

Mr Abdul Hannan: My family friend lived in London and found us a flat to stay in. There were lots of other Bengalis. I stayed with my brothers. We, along with other Bengalis, stayed in the restaurant where we worked. There were four rooms and five of us would share one room at a time, and the restaurant owner would stay in his own room.

Alhaj Abdur Rahman: There were not many Bangladeshi people in Westminster. More Bengalis would stay in the same room as me. However, we would rarely see each other as we all worked at different times. There were times when one room would be occupied by four or five people, but we all worked at different times.

Those who were working in the daytime slept at night, and those who worked at night would sleep in the same bed but during the day. We hardly ever cooked, we would eat bread most of the time or eat at the restaurant. It was tough.

Alhaj Md Abdun Noor: Food was available, we had money to buy things. There would have only been one toilet in a whole building, on the ground floor, and everybody shared it. There were no baths inside the house so we had to go to the public bath once or twice a week.

Haji Arob Ali: It was completely different. During that time the country was nothing like the state it is in now. Toilets and baths did not come with each and every building, we had to go to the public baths. Some households had baths, but the lodgers had no access.

I rented a bed; in each room two beds were available, so two people had to share a room. In Birmingham, three of us shared one room, but in Westminster it was a little bit better as just two people were sharing a room.

Mr Hifzur Rahman: In Bangladesh the houses are very big. My dad's London flat was small with two rooms. Four people slept in one room and two people in another. There was no bathroom, we had to go to the public Marshall Street Baths in Soho. We had to share the toilet with other people in the flat.

Haji Fazar Ali: It was a struggle living in a house with only two rooms, and I had a temporary house in Dagenham. I did not have much help. I found it hard.

Alhaj Muhib Uddin: I had to live here and work in a hotel in Piccadilly. All 11 of us used to work there.

Mr Kobir Miah: Once I arrived in London, there was an issue with accommodation, not just for myself but for everyone. I found a place and I stayed there for many days

At first there were many problems. When I first came, I stayed there for a week and then moved to my uncle's house.

Mr Abdul Moobin: I was surprised to see the living standards of this community. 20-25 people were residing in a cramped house or a flat with very limited facilities. Most of the people were illiterate. They were working in restaurants. It was hard to communicate with them as their use of language was so limited.

Mr Hifzur Rahman: There were few other Bengali houses. In my flat there were around 10-12 people. In my brother-in-law's house there were around 20 Bengalis.

Haji Fazar Ali: In Bangladesh, my whole family stayed in one house, whereas in London in one house it was just me and my dad. I never saw snow in Bangladesh. I saw it in London for the first time.

Mr Fazal Miah: It was not like our country. During that time, there were no baths inside, people had to go to a public bath, and two people slept in one bed. Other than that, people had love and were happy. People usually sent all of their earnings to Bangladesh. However, nowadays people don't do that anymore. Bangladeshi people have lost that sympathy.

> *We wonder if the lack of communication and travel to Bangladesh may be a result of this generation's immediate and extended family living in London - so they do not have the same incentive as the older generation.*

Mr Khalil Miah: No, at that time my wife was doing a course and I was working full-time. In 1979 I moved to Lisson Green with my eldest son. I was given a home with two bedrooms and in 1980 my younger son moved in. At that time, I was working and my wife was doing a course. However, she used to mainly look after the children and when I came back from work, I would help too.

Haji Surok Meah: One of my uncles was here so I joined him at first, but I came alone. The living standards during that time were very poor. My uncle had only one bedroom, and my auntie was with him, so I had to sleep on a sofa.

At the time it was a big problem. Sometimes, 10-15 people lived in one room and most of the time they were either sharing the bed according to their working time or sleeping in the floor. There was no bath so people used to go to the public bath. We would bathe once or twice a week.

Haji Surok Meah: One of my relatives was in Westminster. I liked it there and chose to settle in a rich area; people were very nice and gentle. Many Bengalis tried to settle in Seymour Place but were unable to. During that time I hardly ever went to Lisson Green Estate. I rarely crossed over Marylebone Road.

Unlike single men, it seemed that the situation differed for women - their husbands and family members would often make arrangements for them to have more privacy.

Ms Khaleda Qureshi: Yes, there were some other Bengalis. I had a brother-in-law here. On the day I stepped foot into his house, he was taken to hospital. Sadly he had an asthma attack. There was a grocery shop run by a man named

Patel, so the next day my husband asked him for a room and he said he had one and that we could use it.

He offered us a room with everything - kitchen, sitting room and bed - but the toilet and bath were outside. I came here and lived with my three children in one room. For more than two years we lived like that. Then I moved to Edgware Road, Braithwaite Tower.

Mrs Hosne Ara Moobin: First I stayed at Gloucester Terrace in Westminster. My husband had a flat there so I joined him.

Below you will see the perspectives of the professionals who were / are still involved with the Bangladeshi community.

Ms Karen Buck MP: Westminster was less socially divided than it is now. I mean it has always been a place with very rich areas and much poorer areas - Knightsbridge and Mayfair were always fantastically rich and Church Street and Harrow Road were always poorer.

But I think those extremes have got bigger, because housing is now so expensive that people in the middle are not here so much.

Housing was a problem because Bangladeshi arrivals didn't have money, so tended to need council flats, and there were never enough. It's worse now than it was then, but there was still a lot of overcrowding. That's a problem.

Mr Joe Hegarty: Although the problems in the 70s were bad, lots of people needed housing, the situation was gradually improving. It is different today because the situation is gradually getting worse. The situation in terms of housing was such that people did get opportunities to move.

Because we were in Westminster, the council re-housed people in areas where they wanted. At that time Lisson Green wasn't very popular because, and this dates from when it was created, there was a mix of people from all over.

Everywhere else around here would have been populated by people housed from nearby, so everybody knew each other, whereas there it was more mixed. People on the whole didn't like it. It developed a reputation as a fairly crime-ridden estate.

You had these long interconnected balconies where you could go from house to house. These were removed some time ago but you could get away easily.

It did have a pretty poor reputation, so as a result there were always vacancies, and for people who were coming in desperate for housing it was the most obvious thing.

So the Bangladeshi community started taking shape in Lisson Green. As time moved on and opportunities moved elsewhere, other bits of Church Street were settled by Bangladeshi families as well, but it was initially very much in Lisson Green.

The difference between Church Street and East Marylebone is that you would get single people in East Marylebone because they would come first of all on their own and they would work in the restaurants, rag trade, and so on. When they brought their families over they would get housed in Lisson Green - that was the key to getting housing because you wouldn't get housed here as a single male.

Occupation

The Bangladeshis that settled in Westminster mostly worked within the catering industry. It is often an assumption that Bangladeshis only worked in Indian restaurants. However, we have stories of them working within other cultures as well.

It was also surprising for us to see that individuals had started working from a very early age. The experiences shared here are from a male perspective. Women in the community shared different experiences that will be discussed in the chapter 'Women's stories'.

Alhaj Uster Ali: We didn't have a bathroom or a television, but we didn't care because our focus was to send money back home. I would work the whole week for £5 and out of that I would send £3 to my family in Bangladesh and live off £2. I had to do it because my mum, sisters and brothers were waiting on me to give them money. And that is how I lived.

Haji Surok Meah: I was studying at the time so my intention was to study here. But afterwards I thought it wasn't possible to continue studying without paid employment. Therefore I gave up my studies and I started working in a restaurant.

Mr Guthrie McKie: Bengali men were similar to other groups of people, some skilled but a lot of unskilled. A lot of the unskilled would either end up working on the buses or in other important unskilled work. It was often not well paid - they could be working for the council, street cleaning. Important work but not well paid. For those who were unskilled, with no trade or profession, it meant that they would experience high levels of poverty for years to come, which would often be later handed on to their children.

Haji Arob Ali: For two months I was in Birmingham but could not find a job. I then moved to Westminster and started working at a restaurant. It was an English restaurant and I have since always worked in English restaurants.

I went to Birmingham hoping to get a job in a factory, but they were all closing down so I could not find anything. Restaurant jobs were available in Westminster, so many people from outside Westminster started to come here. One of my cousins was already here and he asked me to come.

Alhaj Abdur Rahman: I was always living in Westminster. I came on November 1 and during my first 2-3 days, I was very happy; I thought at least I am in London. But at the same time I was also worried about my future.

What I will be able to do? For around 10-11 days I was unemployed. I continued to ask people. They showed me the places that I should go and how I should approach employers. I learnt one sentence and repeated that to each potential employer: 'I am looking for a job'. Eventually I got a job in a restaurant in Marylebone Station. The manager was so nice he offered me long hours. During that time, normal working hours was 48 hours a week. I did two shifts and six days in a week.

Mr Abdul Sobur: I came when I was 10 or 12, and started working straight away. When I came to this country I already had a cousin here, who'd arrived in 1957. He was working as a chef in an Italian restaurant in Paddington.

I think around five or six weeks after I'd arrived, my cousin talked to the manager of the restaurant and got me a job at the same place. I continued to work here and there until I had learnt the skills for the job. During that time, there was one owner and one manager.

After this, I was taken to a different restaurant near Victoria and I worked there for about a year. After that I came back to King's Cross and worked at a restaurant on the King's Cross Road for another year or two.

Ms Syeda Chowdhury: My husband's uncle had a restaurant here and my husband was working as a waiter in a restaurant near Charing Cross. I used to stay alone in Sidcup in the flat above the restaurant. Downstairs there were Bengali people.

Mr Abdul Hannan: When I first got to the UK, I had to sell curry and rice for a living.

Mr Khalil Miah: No, there were some Bengalis, but there were not as many families. And the families that were here, the parents were not around because they were always working.

I got a part time job to make money. I travelled eight miles for a job which paid me £4. I also worked in an Indian restaurant. Although I was interested in this country, I always wanted to return to Bangladesh.

After two years, I pressured my dad to send me to Bangladesh so he bought me a ticket and I stayed in Bangladesh for about 8-9 months, maybe even 12.

Ms Karen Buck MP: Jobs. It is still true that a British Bangladeshi is going to find it harder to get work, at least well-paid work, than many other minority communities. That was a real problem and still is. The community has come a long way educationally, but there is still a problem with housing and still a problem with equal opportunities for well-paid work.

It was difficult getting reasonably paid work. What you had for a lot of new arrival Bangladeshi communities in London was different to Manchester or the Pakistani communities in some of the mill towns, where there were particular types of employment.

Some of those employers were deliberately going to other countries to recruit workers to come. In central London, that was a bit different because you don't have that single industry that you have elsewhere. But obviously the catering industry was a really big deal for the Bangladeshi community and it still is a big deal.

So a lot of people came and were working in and around the catering industry. But then, a lot of people don't want that for their own children - that's again part of the immigrant story. They will do everything they have to do and they will work until they drop, but they will want their children to get on and do something different.

I think the communities of the 60s, 70s and 80s were working very, very hard in particular industries, with the restaurant trade being a really big part of that. That has changed – although there is still a very successful curry industry, a lot of young Bangladeshis don't want to work in the restaurant trade, so you have those issues.

Mr Joe Hegarty: There were lots of Asians who were part of the community of people who moved here in the early to mid-70s, but at that time it was not a largely Bengali community.

They were a minority so it was very mixed. They would have been a substantial minority but gradually, in the late 70s and early 80s, people moved on and vacancies arose.

There was a large Bengali community in East Marylebone for two reasons: because there were a lot of restaurants in that area, and a lot of Bangladeshi people came to work in those restaurants. Additionally, because the rag trade still existed in those days, a lot of Bangladeshi people worked in that. So they tended to come and live with families in very overcrowded accommodation.

Mr Guthrie McKie: It tended to be the grocer's shops, and there is a cultural difference if you look at South Indian or Sri Lankan shopkeepers. They tend to replicate what white shopkeepers used to sell, whereas when you get to Bangladeshi and Arab shops, they tend to move off into a specific type of food that they sell, although it's hard to tell them that.

They think there's still a market here for that type of retail outlet, but it is disappearing. So Bengalis started with a retail outlet which was very, very specific to their community, which was different from other immigrants from the Asian subcontinent, who tended to replicate what the British were doing.

Alhaj Uster Ali: When I first came to Westminster I worked in a canteen but it was a fixing job, so I asked the station manager, who I knew well, how I could get another job. He told me to fill out an application and sit an interview, which I did, and that's how I first started working for British Rail.

I had many jobs at British Rail, from working as a forklift driver to working in the Red Star Parcels office. There I was my own supervisor, I would hand over parcels to those who had bought their identification.

Mrs Hosne Ara Moobin: My husband mostly worked in an office or a related field. People would often ask him for help, even now he is still helping people in the community.

Mr Abdul Moobin: I enrolled at a college in order to qualify as a chartered account, as my visa was not a student visa - it was a voucher - which meant I could work here as well. At the time, I thought that if I applied only for the student visa I may be restricted to work, therefore I obtained a voucher.

Adjusting to Britain

Alhaj Md Abdun Noor: I did not feel comfortable here, and at first I decided that I would return to Bangladesh after a short period of time. This country was nice, no doubt about it, but I missed my country. The weather was very different; it was very cold, whereas in my country the weather was hot.

Mr Abdul Hannan: There were no similarities to Bangladesh; the cars, even the food, it was all different. People were really caring here and took care of each other in those days. Some days it would rain and on other days the weather was good. In comparison to Bangladesh, the UK had a bit of everything.

Alhaj Lala Miah: It felt hard to adjust. First of all, the weather was completely different. It was usually foggy, dark and full of snow. We rarely saw sunny days. It was really hard to cope. That was a very difficult time but slowly I adjusted.

Haji Arob Ali: Not bad. I come from a remote area where there is not much to do except cultivate. I had never been in a city, so it was new to me and I hoped to have a good job.

Ms Azizun Khatun: The biggest difference that I noticed was the freedom of choice. At that time in Bangladesh we were not able to do things as freely as we were able to do here - although the situation has changed now. The weather was very cold; when I came it was snowing, for almost a month it was full of snow.

Mr Abdul Moobin: The environment was completely different, the law and order was very strict, even the transport was more regulated. Things came on time and people were happy to queue. Everyone was very honest at the time. It was very nice; everything was clean and tidy.

Mr Kobir Miah: This country felt very strange, the people functioned in a different way to what I was used to. People were driving cars and wore different clothes, which I was not used to. Also the weather was very cold, really cold. I came in February and I can remember it being very windy and cold. It took a while to get from London Euston to Manchester and the journey was very cold.

Mrs Hosne Ara Moobin: I had no relatives, no friends or close members of the family here, so initially I felt lonely, but I slowly overcame this. The weather was different. It was very cold but I enjoyed the weather here as it was the first time I had seen snow and the cold climate. It looks nice, so often I went out to see the beauty of the weather.

The cooking facilities were also completely different. In our country, accessing electricity was not as straightforward and we rarely owned cookers etc. Many things were rare in our country; the standard of living in this country was completely different and nicer than our country so I liked that.

Alhaj Lala Miah: I can still remember those days - we would need to wear many layers of clothing in order to stay warm. We would need to wrap our whole body with clothes before we would go outside, we would even wear two pairs of socks in order to protect ourselves from the cold.

It was mostly foggy. When we first came in this country, many of the things were not as they are now, such as the streets, housing, heating and even baths and toilets; they were completely different. Westminster has improved a lot since then.

Alhaj Uster Ali: There was nobody from my province in Bangladesh, but there were some people who I had a distant relationship with.

I didn't understand the language, I had problems getting work, and Bangladeshis faced major problems. We had rooms with no doors - in one room there would be 5-7 people sleeping.

10-15 people would eat rice with one curry out of one pot. Not like today. Later on, once we slowly learnt the language, we could stand on our own feet.

The way of life was different in this country. Travelling from one city to another was a real struggle. We were illiterate and did not understand this culture. A lot of us did not know how to read numbers so what we used to do was put bricks in front of our homes to signal our location.

My friend did not know what 'eight' was, so I told him 'put two eggs on top of each other, and the number which looks like that is an eight'.

Ms Noorjahan Begum: It was not bad. At first, we went to a hotel then we were taken to a council house. During that time housing options were very impressive, they re-housed us in hostels. We were welcomed by Bengalis as well as English people. At that time there were quite a few Bengalis here and there. In Paddington there were only 5-6 families.

Mr Guthrie McKie: I think there was a great difficulty. There were great barriers if you look at the way people in the mainstream community communicate and meet each other. This is the advantage the Afro-Caribbean community had - they had no trouble going into a pub, that's where you met British people; they had no trouble going to parties or whatever it was.

That was very difficult for the Bengali community, many of whom just wouldn't go to a pub, which meant that there was an area of contact that they would not be part of. The majority of the population wrongly interpreted that as people deliberately isolating themselves.

It was a wrong interpretation but it was the way they saw it – here's a community that doesn't want to interact with us. That lack of ability to understand each other fed from the fact there was a community which, for cultural and religious reasons, had a different way of communicating.

Difficulties during the 1960s & 1970s

People spoke to us about their worries about 'skinheads' and incidences of physical violence. Not everybody was directly affected but, within a lot of these difficult stories, a sense of support and community comes through as people came together to deal with their difficulties.

Mr Guthrie McKie: Well, Harrow Road, the area I represent, has a long history of Afro-Caribbean immigration. That's known as North Paddington and it was only in the 70s that the Bangladeshi community moved into that part.

So in some ways, they benefited from the fact that the Afro-Caribbean community took the brunt of all the discrimination, that by the time the Bangladeshi community arrived, the discrimination hadn't disappeared, of course it hadn't, but it wasn't as brutal as it was. That's when the Bangladeshi community started up small businesses.

Mr Abdul Sobur: No, fortunately it never happened to me. God saved me from this. I was living in Westbourne Grove at the time. I used to walk home with another person. This one time, when we came to the end of the road where our restaurant was located, where there was a tall building with glass windows, there were approximately 25 skinheads waiting on that corner. When cars were driving towards them, they'd just turn around and take an alternative route, but for us there was no alternative route, we had to walk past that corner.

A few people had warned me not to use this route. All I said was that I have no choice. There were concerns that if we would take that route, we would get beaten up. Instead, I told my friend to walk behind me and keep his eyes to himself, not to look left or right.

I prepared him, told him that if one of them pushes him, to make sure he falls onto another one of them. We started walking fast to avoid all this, then we went past them and 10 of them started walking after us while 15 waited behind.

Then, as we were walking, we saw bottles being thrown. My friend told me to stop watching and run as they would come for us, so we ran home. After a few days, all the glass windows of the building had been smashed. That's the only time I came close to falling into trouble, otherwise I was safe.

Haji Arob Ali: I was hoping for a job and a better life, but during that time, the situation of this country was not as it is now. There was often violence and racial attacks. Therefore, we always feared that at any time something bad could happen. Especially during the nights, when we'd return from work, there would usually be two or three of us together.

Mr Hifzur Rahman: When I had the St John's Wood flat, we had an English couple living downstairs, our neighbours. The flat had wooden flooring and my children were young. They made a lot of noise which the downstairs neighbours could hear. They gave me a lot of problems about this and there were a lot of complaints.

I told the council that after 9pm there should be no noise and I put my children to bed before 9pm. I found my downstairs neighbours were racist. I had a good relationship with all my other neighbours once the council removed them from the house.

Mr Abdul Hannan: Whilst doing my overtime, my manager said I can leave early and he would still pay me. As I was leaving in my work clothes a white man approached me and threw me on the floor and hit me.

I went back into work and I remember the customers saying that a dirty man had come in and the staff needed to tell him to leave. But the staff took me to the hospital straightaway. Nowadays, it is more multicultural in Westminster and these types of things don't happen anymore.

Mr Hifzur Rahman: There weren't many difficulties. When you went outside, communication was important, but as I learned, it was not a problem. The main difficulty was a group of people known as 'skinheads', who were racist. When they were around I would avoid going outside. I was fearful of that.

Mrs Harisun Nessa: I struggled during those days. The hotel we stayed at didn't have facilities for me to cook. We had to order food from restaurants. It was expensive, even for one meal, so we would order out for one meal and then have bread, on its own.

Alhaj Muhib Uddin: Every day I would feel like I wanted to go back to Bangladesh. Especially every morning when I woke up. I couldn't open the house door and the water would not come out from the taps because it used to be so cold that everything used to get very icy. I was always having to fix things and clean stuff up.

Bangladesh was warmer. Twice I got into trouble and had to pay a fine.

Before I went to sleep every night I would make sure I put aside how much each of my children would need for bus fare and food. If I did not have the money I would not be able to sleep.

Alhaj Lala Miah: In 1977 my family eventually joined me in the UK. At the time, I had a flat in Lisson Green. That was the first time I faced any racial abuse. There were times when I felt very insecure on my way to work; there was no certainty that I would return safely.

It wasn't just me; lots of others also felt the same. Our family members would eagerly wait for our safe return. There were times they would be looking at the street to see whether we would be coming back without any trouble.

There were no mobile phones back then, so we couldn't inform our family that we were on our way. They waited for us for hours and hours. The most abuse we received was usually in front of lifts. Racist people would loiter in front of the lifts and assault vulnerable people.

There was a lot of crime in the Lisson Green area; I was victimised and many others were even attacked. The authorities were good; they took action against those types of incidents. Things have changed. Nowadays we are very comfortable in this area.

Mr Abdul Moobin: My only difficulty was looking for appropriate advice - where to get a job.

Alhaj Uster Ali: When I first landed at Heathrow I thought to myself, this is a white person's country. It was very strange because this was an unfamiliar sight. When I left the airport I was given an address which took me to North West London, Daventry Street.

I stayed there for a week and then left for Birmingham because I had some relatives there. Coming to this country, I never knew about racism. There were so many problems, white people used to attack blacks and my community also faced this problem; we really had to struggle and fight to stay in this country.

I thought London would be good, although I didn't ever think I would see white people spit on black people and because of this, I really suffered. This country was very problematic but I was a really strong man, I was six feet tall and weighed 16 stone.

I became established. I had my own coffee bar in Birmingham. God willing, I was able to help my fellow Bengalis, especially those who were scared of being attacked by the locals. In our area, there were lots of skinheads who would target Bengalis.

Mr Abdul Sobur: My son, who was five years old, was enrolled at a school near Harrow Road. The school was predominately white; a friend of mine also sent his children there. Along with his children, he took my son, because I was at work and the children needed to be dropped off and collected. My son was five and his son was seven. One time, these white boys came to my son and my friend's son and grabbed their arms and punched him in his nose. My friend informed the teacher, who was also white, who laughed when told.

I decided to remove my son from the school to one closer to me - St Augustine's Primary School, which is also a secondary school now. At the time, lot of people I knew opposed the idea of him moving. That school had predominantly black children; he continued to get into fights and get hurt.

But I said, he was already involved in fights, if I put him here and it happens again, then that's just how it is. What else can I do? I'll just change his school again if I need to.

Once I had him enrolled, I realised it wasn't just black children; there were other races too - such as Moroccan children. Even till this day, I have not heard people tell me that the school is known for fighting.

Mr Fazal Miah: Once I was attacked and they wanted my money. When he took out his dagger, I kicked him and ran away. Nearby an Iraqi helped me and sheltered me.

Ms Syeda Chowdhury: Not really many difficulties except for one day. A man came and snatched my bag from me, and inside were my keys. I was very scared and didn't know how I would collect my child. My husband had the other set of keys.

I went to our local corner shop - which was run by an Indian man – and I explained my situation, that I had no keys and needed to collect my children. He told me not to worry and that he would help me. He asked me where my husband worked. I said my husband works in Baker Street (back then my husband worked in the ticket office at Baker Street Station), so the man took me to Baker Street so that I could find my husband and explain the situation. The man took me back with his car.

Fortunately, I had already told someone else to collect my children and look after them until I was able to return. So they took care of my children until I'd returned from my husband's work place.

Mr Joe Hegarty: I don't recall it being a major problem when I was a councillor. I do remember tensions and violence earlier between white and black people, but I don't remember so much with the Bengali community.

The racism wasn't like that; all the authorities were run by white people, all the institutions were ruled by white people. So it was in the institutional side of things that racism was experienced.

People didn't get a fair deal in things like education. They came eventually but it took a fair while for things like ESOL classes and eventually home language classes, which were introduced in the 80s. Things like that started to happen but it took a while.

Mr Guthrie McKie: My experience of Westminster and immigration was that the black Caribbean community has the toughest time. The discrimination against black people in the 50s and 60s was horrendous; it was unbelievable.

I don't believe the Bangladeshi community has experienced anything like that. I've still got some Jamaican friends and it was nothing like the discrimination they experienced 30 or 40 years ago.

Mr Khalil Miah: I didn't have the burden of sending money back to Bangladesh, since I lived together with my father, uncles and cousins. Out of the whole family I was the youngest so I had no pressure to send money, nor did anybody pressure me. In fact, they paid for me to go Bangladesh. So I was really comfortable.

There was one time when I did struggle, but just a little. I didn't really know how to work so I moved from job to job. It was okay because I had my father and uncle.

However, when my wife came over, I had my first son. I had to get a job with plenty of hours which I could not leave. In the past, I had worked for 3-4 months, but when my wife came, I had to keep the job for longer. My wife is a really nice woman, she gave me plenty of guidance. Through our debates she has helped me adapt to this culture.

Dr Andrew Elder: I think the thing I was most aware of was the very different ways of understanding health. The way they used us as doctors was very different from other communities, and there is quite a lot to learn about that.

I think you have to remember that, as a GP in that area of London, it wasn't only the Bengalis who were new there. We were dealing with a highly multi-ethnic community with people from all kinds of backgrounds. Learning more about the lives people had led before coming to Marylebone was always very important to establish a relationship. In the 80s and 90s, there were masses of refugees from the Yugoslav wars and people from all over the world arriving in Westminster.

The thing that occurs to me is racism, and I do remember episodes of racism for patients. I don't actually remember any instances for the Bengali community, but I remember a West Indian patient being very badly beaten up in a racist attack on the Lisson Green estate, so one was always aware of racism. I don't know that I spoke often about racism to Bengali patients.

Education was a problem. I remember pressures on Gateway School, which became an almost completely Bengali school. Those are just some of the things.

Chapter four

Languages

Although it was a barrier to integration for the Bengali community, language helped unite the Bengali diasporas at that time. People encountered many difficulties due to language barriers, and we have heard many different journeys that people took in order to learn the English language.

Bangladeshi migrants who understood English would often act as ambassadors and advisors within the community, helping others to fill in forms and access the services they needed.

Barriers

Mr Mohammed Siraj: In the Bengali community in the area, when people first came over, what I noticed was that they could not speak English at all.

At that time there was a big, big problem - communication. They tend to stick together for that purpose. They used to frequently visit the shops where there was someone who can speak to them in their language or talk to them in a way they could understand (Hindi or Urdu).

Ms Khaleda Qureshi: When I came to Westminster I was not able to speak or understand any English. But whatever language problems we had at the beginning, we overcame them. In the beginning I'd only say 'Yes' or 'No'. I only went to primary school in Bangladesh - my father never allowed girls to enter further education. I was never brought up in the city either, which made things more difficult for me, but my husband helped me a lot during that time.

Mrs Hosne Ara Moobi: It was a new country and a different language - our language is Bengali. Although I studied English it was not the spoken version, so I was worried that it would be difficult in the UK. I was a little worried, but not too much, as knowing some English gave me some confidence.

I studied English. I could speak but I didn't feel like I could have a conversation in English, as I have never interacted using the English language in my own country. Slowly I realized that my spoken English had to improve if I was to live in this country.

I usually communicated with people using simple English. I was hesitant and lacked confidence, not like nowadays. I never went to any classes.

Ms Azizun Khatun: My biggest problem was the English language; I couldn't speak it so I felt embarrassed. We had Indian neighbours, who once invited me to their home. I felt a little bit more comfortable there and would occasionally visit them.

My father-in-law realised that I was unhappy because of the language barriers. He said that he had spent most of his life in England without English, so why had I become so unhappy over a short period of time? He assured me that he would send me to English classes to learn English.

Ms Azizun Khatun: The main difficulty was the language. I could not express myself! I was unable to share things, even issues with my health. There was nobody my age except my neighbour, who was Indian. To manage this better I enrolled at a school, but later dropped out to manage the household chores. When I was away my mother-in-law had to cook and clean the house, which seemed strange to me. For me, caring for my in-laws was more important than my studies.

Mr Abdul Moobin: English was not a problem for us. The issue was with fluency of the local dialects. In addition to this, people from Bangladesh had a poor knowledge of this country's system, so I could not seek any help from them and had to do most things alone.

Mr Kobir Miah: In primary school I studied English grammar. When I went to the airport the immigration officer asked me, 'Can you speak English?' and I did not understand. Then he asked me 'Do you know English?' and I said 'No'. With the very little English I understood, when he said 'Do you know English?', I knew what to reply.

Ms Khaleda Qureshi: I first came to Westminster and stayed here for two days, then I was taken to Manchester. I was not feeling well so the following day I was taken to the hospital by Lucie, a family friend and neighbour. I was admitted to the hospital but I didn't know what was going on.

Lucie took me to a room and changed my clothes. She spoke to me but I did not understand. She then left and I waited for her to return but she did not. Doctors and nurses started to see me. I did not understand what they were saying and I could not communicate, so I started crying. I was taken care of, but I was upset. When my husband finally arrived in the evening, I felt so relieved.

Mr Guthrie McKie: I think it manifested itself in people not understanding each other. If you don't have a dialogue with people it becomes difficult to understand what each other's position or point of view is. If a Bengali man had poor English and strong religious views then of course he deliberately didn't mix – a) because he didn't speak the language and b) because they (non-Muslim people) tended to go to the pub and parties, which is something a Muslim wouldn't do. Isolation probably increased considerably for that first generation.

Ms Noorjahan Begum: Language was the main barrier during that time. Even I myself did some interpreting for our Bengali women during that time.

Dr Andrew Elder: Yes, I think so. In the early days we were very worried about the children of Bengali families being used as interpreters. Custom has changed a great deal now, there are professional interpreters, but in the early days we often had members of the family who acted as interpreters.

In fact, I remember there was a nine-year-old in a family who I got to know quite well because their English was quite good and they liked to chat, and they seemed to be a kind of ambassador. They were in school!

They were the ambassadors for their family when it came to dealing with doctors, other community things, social security offices, whatever they had to do. As doctors we were worried about the pressures on nine- and 10-year-olds, and whether they were being kept out of school to do these things.

Dr Andrew Elder: Obviously, language was the biggest barrier. If you wanted to find out what was going on in a family, you had a barrier of language but you also had a barrier of social custom, and what the family might feel uncomfortable talking about.

I probably did notice that there was quite a difference between men and women. I had much less access to what was happening with the women, with the men being in control of bringing people to the doctors and things.

Opportunity

Alhaj Md Abdun Noor: After completing my education, I came to this country. I was able to speak a little English. In order to improve even further, I enrolled at Putney College. I was working at the same time. After about three or four months it became very difficult and I could not carry on any more. However, by this point I had sufficient English to manage myself.

Mr Khalil Miah: I learnt English through daily interactions but I also went to language school, which helped.

Mr Abdul Hannan: My older brother was already in this country and he enrolled me at a school to learn the language. Slowly I learned how to speak English. At first there were problems in communication with English people but then I was fine, although I did have my brother to help with translation.

Ms Khaleda Qureshi: Mostly, my husband took me to doctors or any other appointments. He normally told me how to speak and what to say. But most of the language I picked up from my children when they started school. I never took any English classes, I just interacted with children and watched TV and spoke with neighbours.

The community elders helped us during this period. Though we were not able to speak English, they tried to understand what we were trying to say. Whenever I went out with my children, they always talked to the locals. I always avoided this interaction as I did not understand the language. However, I did get along with my neighbours.

Haji Fazar Ali: I did not understand anything. I slowly began to learn things once my dad took me to school. Bangladesh and England are very different. There were four Bengalis in school. We helped each other out and would communicate with non-Bengalis together.

Ms Noorjahan Begum: I could not speak English but I had my own methods. For example, I would gesture with my hands when interacting.

Mr Hifzur Rahman: I worked at first and did not know much English. Working in a shop I had to deal with a lot of African and English customers. There were very few Bengali customers, so I had to speak English, a lot. Through this my English improved.

Whilst I was in Bangladesh my teacher said, if you're going to London then you will need to be able to speak English. So I attended English class in Bangladesh for six months. The school I attended in England helped me communicate as well as work in the shop.

Haji Arob Ali: I learnt some English, but I had Bengali colleagues at work who would help to translate.

Haji Surok Meah: I learnt English here. I told my manager that I wished to work as a waiter. Wages for a waiter were only £7, whereas a chef's wage was £13. He asked me if I agreed to this or not? I agreed. My intention was to become a businessman. I already became a chef but I needed to be experienced as a waiter. One day, I would be the owner of a business so I needed these skills.

Alhaj Lala Miah: I was able to understand English people and was able to communicate with them, as my job as a waiter helped me improve my language skills.

I never sought any help from anyone when visiting doctors etc. I tried my best to do those things myself. The people of this country are very intelligent. They easily understand what you are trying to say.

Mr Joe Hegarty: The English language skills of Bengali people became a lot better, as almost all families had access to at least someone who could speak English, even if the person who actually needed things didn't.

Alhaj Muhib Uddin: I did not have time to go to school as I had to work to provide for my family, and that's where I learned English, very gradually.

At first I could not speak English at all, even with

doctors. However, if you said a few basic words, they would understand what I was saying.

Mr Joe Hegarty: As far as I was concerned, communication was often through mediators, the people who were more articulate within the community. That tended to be it at the beginning, but then kids started to mediate (translate, interpret) afterwards.

It can be inappropriate for kids to translate certain things, not for the things I was doing but obviously for medical conditions etc. Over the years the medical profession began to get translators and translation services, even if it was over the telephone.

Chapter five

Home away from home

Keeping it Halal

As second and third generation British Bangladeshis, we have been bought up with Bangladeshi cuisine available at home whenever we want it. For us it has become the norm to have access to the rich foods of Bangladesh.

However, this quality cuisine was not as accessible for first generation migrants! In fact, it was this generation's passion for food that brought the curry to British shores and made it possible for us to have this beautiful part of our roots so present in our everyday lives.

Haji Surok Meah: We had problems with food as at that time as it was not easy to get halal food. Even the restaurant manager was not bothered about it. I'd normally eat eggs and potatoes. I must say that we had many difficulties during that time.

Ms Azizun Khatun: We could get halal food but it was not available locally. Our elders always collected halal food from Aldgate.

Mr Abdul Moobin: There was a halal shop in Drummond Street. I used to get halal chicken or meat.

Alhaj Muhib Uddin: There was no halal food at that time. There was no rice either, just the rice pudding rice which we could not eat the way we eat our Bangladeshi type of food. So I would just eat bread and eggs.

Alhaj Uster Ali: We used to buy a chicken for 20p and it used to last us the whole week. We used to buy a bag of rice and that used to last us.

Mr Abdul Hannan: I could find some halal food as I knew some settled Bengali Muslims already.

Mrs Anowara Begum: I could cook but not everything, but my husband always showed me how to cook here and brought all the types of spices for me.

> *It is interesting that a male was showing the woman how to cook.*

Mrs Anowara Begum: Halal was not available locally so he purchased it from Aldgate. There was a shop in Seymour

Place, you could occasionally get halal from there, but he mostly went to the market in Aldgate.

On Eid day, I made pita (dumplings) and other Bangladeshi foods that we'd eat together. I always preferred my children to be dressed up in a salwar kameez, and as they were rare at the time, I would make them for them myself. They may have been available somewhere else at the time, but nowhere that I knew about. For my boys, I always ordered Panjabi from Bangladesh. On Eid day, I invited my neighbours and fed them and their children- they were always welcome in my home.

Mr Khalil Miah: In terms of food my wife used to cook and my eldest daughter would also help. I used to work in a restaurant so I had an interest in cooking, so I helped when I could. In 1967, when we first came, there was halal food and halal shops, and the workers in restaurants used to eat in those restaurants. I used to mainly eat in the restaurant and on my days off, I used to eat at home with my wife.

Alhaj Md Abdun Noor: There was halal food in Aldgate or Crompton Street. We went there to buy meat from Mr Noor Miah's shop. People usually pronounced it 'Noor Miar shop'. An English woman also ran a live chicken shop, so every Sunday we would buy chicken from there and slaughter them ourselves.

Alhaj Lala Miah: No halal food was easily accessible, only rice, vegetables and fish. Although the fish was not from Bangladesh, it was mostly English fish. We got fresh chicken from Hessel Street in Aldgate.

Haji Arob Ali: It was very difficult to find halal food in this area. The only halal food was available in Aldgate. So sometimes we bought halal from there on Sundays. As a restaurant worker, I only cooked twice a week. In London, two or three people working together and residing in a household would share the food. We bought three or four weeks' worth of halal meat from Aldgate and cooked a portion each week.

Ms Khaleda Qureshi: In those days, most of the houses were old and the toilets were outside. There were no baths in the house so we would have to go to public baths. A lot of things were so different to Bangladesh. The one thing I do remember is that my husband bought chickens every week, and they looked like they were from Bangladesh. At that time Bombay Duck was very popular. I would fry up some Bombay Duck for my meal. I was not used to the meat during that time, and I'm still not.

My husband once asked me to do a Kurma Pilau on Eid day. He bought all the right spices. Ghee wasn't available during those days so he bought butter instead. He would always invite his friends to have their meal with us.

Mr Abdul Sobur: There were two grocery shops on Drummond Street and they used to claim that their meat was halal. But once I saw a man butchering and I went and saw the way in which the butchering was happening - it wasn't done properly. Honestly, they never gave us halal food, but had said it was halal and sold it to us.

Ms Syeda Chowdhury: No, there wasn't much. One day I asked the shopkeeper if there was any rice powder, as I wanted to make pita (a traditional Bengali bread). He bought me a packet, and I took it home and made the pita. At the time I was in Sidcup. The people who worked at the restaurant were surprised and asked how I had come across the pita. They said they weren't able to get it there. I went and got more and fed everyone and they happily ate it. It had been many years since we ate pita.

In terms of fish, there was mainly 'roe' fish available. We didn't know what country it was from. People used to tell me that it came from America. So yes it was mainly roe fish and hardly anything else. I barely ate chicken or meat, I usually ate fish.

The men ate chicken and meat, although they didn't really know whether it was halal or not. When people first came it was hard to know what was halal anyway. I used to have a lot of vegetables and prawns too.

Mr Guthrie McKie: I think my very first one was in the early 60s when my friend took me for what was then called an Indian. I'd never been for an Indian! I'll always remember that first experience.

I fell in love with curry! I think that's the experience of a lot of British white people. That's the first experience you have - the food. Once the food seduces you, that's it. It's a very important route into understanding the culture.

Clothes

Unlike Bangladeshi men, who largely adopted British clothing, women were more likely to continue wearing traditional outfits such as the saree or salwar kameez. Just as they have been able to preserve traditional Bangladeshi food, they ensured traditional garments are easily accessible for our generation.

Mrs Anowara Begum: I always wore sarees, I never dropped my culture. When I was a school student I used to wear the salwar kameez. My father encouraged me to wear a saree, he loved it, so to keep him in my memories I would wear a saree.

I worked in a school for a long time with my saree, and never faced any problems. I have not seen any negative feelings amongst my colleagues or other people. No one raised an issue with me. I had previously rarely covered my head or wore the burka, but after hajj I started to cover my head and started wearing a burka.

Mrs Hosne Ara Moobin: I always wore sarees, even whilst I was employed, along with other clothes to cope with the cold. Recently I started wearing trousers with a kameez as I have to look after my husband and accompany him to hospital or doctor's appointments etc. This type of dress is convenient.

Ms Azizun Khatun: At that time, the tradition of this country was to wear either shirts, pants or a skirt, no Muslim dresses were available. Those who were with their parents-in-law would have to follow their instructions. They were not willing to allow western clothing. So I managed in a saree.

The interviewer asked if she ever wore any western clothing.

Mrs Harisun Nessa: (Laughs) I have only ever worn my saree's. I even wore my hijab.

I never had anyone ask or approach about what I was wearing.

Ms Khaleda Qureshi: I always wore sarees, I never changed my tradition. On top of the saree, of course I used to wear coats or cardigans to protect myself from the cold, but never without the saree. English people always looked at me because of the saree.

Mr Abdul Moobin: I always wore suits and overcoats. Just like the western way of life.

Haji Arob Ali: Coat, pants and other warm clothes for outside, but at home we wore a lungi and shirt. It was always cold but in London I feel less cold compared to outside London. Birmingham temperatures used to be lower than London, so the people of Birmingham had more warm clothes than us, such as overcoat etc.

Mr Kobir Miah: Of course it was different clothes. At that time, people used to wear ties and suits. When people used to go outside, they would wear smart clothes.

Mr Khalil Miah: I had style back then and I still have style today (giggles); my life was stylish. I have a beard, I pray namaaz (Islamic prayer), no problem, but also I have always worn expensive suits and shoes. Now I have children and nine grandchildren. My grandchildren like the way I dress and I just tell them this is my habit.

The community

One of the most powerful themes that we identified from our interviews was how supportive the Bangladeshi community was to one another. The Bangladeshi culture is collectivist, and Bangladeshi migrants brought that with them to London.

They would openly approach other Bangladeshis to offer their support and share what little they had. Their stories share themes such as trust, loyalty, respect and care for the community and neighbours - traits we feel are gradually being lost as we become a generation more concerned with our own needs and that of our immediate families.

Alhaj Md Abdun Noor: Five or six people were in the same building with my brother, and two or three Bengali families were nearby. At that time, many people were there.

Ms Karen Buck MP: Well I think what we know about new arrival communities is that all of them have a tendency to go to where there is already a small community. So you only need a few people for new arrivals to go to where they are.

In the beginning, new arrival communities were quite insecure and they liked to have the comfort of being around a community that is like them, and also has memories and a past and support for each other. That's not unusual for Bangladeshi communities; it's true for all communities.

As the communities get more settled and usually a bit better off, then it will become more mixed and people will go to different places. And another thing is that new communities go to where housing is cheap, and that changes, so nothing stays the same.

Mr Mohammed Siraj: Major problem was the language and the lack of communication, and that led to more problems.

Mrs Harisun Nessa: Bengalis moved to the area much later on. One day much after I had settled into the country, my husband introduced me to a Bengali lady he met, Hajirah, who I thought dressed like a man (western clothing). (laughs) She was in western clothing, so we spoke a little bit.

Me and my friend had heard that a new family had settled into the area. We found out where they lived and went to visit them. We knocked on the door and a man answered asking us why we had come. We told him we were from the area and that we heard about them recently moving in. We asked if they had settled in ok, and where they were from in Bangladesh. They seemed pleased to see us.

How about any cultural differences?

There were cultural differences but they used to overcome them with being together. They could go to each other's places or minor community centres.

Bengalis tend to keep to themselves rather than mingle with other communities, that I have noticed. So there was not that much interaction with the different communities there.

Haji Fazar Ali: There were a lot of Bengalis in the area.

Mr Abdul Hannan: I thought I would get lots of help as a lot of my family was already here. My family gave me £5-10 here and there, and also some clothes.

Alhaj Abdur Rahman: Barrister Abbas Ali even told me that if I continued my education here, I would be able to do better things.

But my mind worked differently, I just thought of ways to earn more money. I'd always received letters from back home with demands to send money and buy land. Sometimes, my hands would be empty, but my roommates were so helpful, they would offer me loans to meet my family's demands.

I never asked for it, they would do it willingly, they offered me as much as they could. During that time we were all very generous; we had so much affection towards each other, even more than if they were our own brothers. I had some other side business as well. All the members of my household used to send money home through me.

They gave whatever amount they wanted to send off, and I took this money and sent it through the United Bank Ltd, during the period of Pakistani rule, now it's called Janata Bank. The manager of this Bank was a Pakistani man; he noticed that I was always sending money. He kindly made a deal with me where I earn £1 on every hundred pounds. He also asked other colleagues to count transactions under my name, so monthly I would receive approximately £25-30 from him. It was lot during that time. I was able to cover my personal costs with this money and send my net wages to Bangladesh.

Ms Syeda Chowdhury: There used to be Bengali males but not many Bengali females. I used to sit down and relax, and when the restaurant wasn't busy I'd go there and everyone there I'd call uncle and they'd all treat me like their niece, they'd always feed me and treat me with something if they went out.

No, there weren't many Bengalis there but there was this one lady, very light skinned, who I saw from a distance once, and then I ended up moving near her. Then once in the street we saw each other and she was wearing a saree so I spoke to her, and she asked me which country are you from?

I said Bangladesh. That moment she gave me a massive hug and said she hasn't found another Bengali person and she has been here for a few months. So I used to go to her house a lot and she used to care about me a lot and treated me like her sister. If she cooked she would make it for me too, I did cook occasionally too.

Mrs Hosne Ara Moobin: No, there were no Bengalis nearby. Some of them were in Westminster but not near us. We had some friends in Baker Street. We always kept in contact with each other. Once every week or two we would meet and spend time together.

Mr Fazal Miah: I came to Westminster after having my family with me, say about 1969. Westminster was very good at that time. I had a relative in Dudley House, he sheltered me there with my family.

Ms Azizun Khatun: Not many Bengali families were here, I have seen only three families near us. We would hardly see any Bengalis outside either.

Alhaj Uster Ali: I also helped start a community. I am one of the founders of the Marylebone Bangladesh Society. We had about 500 members. Every building had about four or five families. However, in the 70s, there were only three or four Bengali families in Lisson Green.

Mr Fazal Miah: None of my family members were here. I had a cousin in Scotland. Only two Bengali families were near us.

Alhaj Lala Miah: No way was I able to know everything or understand everything. It has taken time to learn many things. Slowly I started to use buses, trains etc, but I have to say that the people of this country were very helpful.

No, there were not many Bengali people in Westminster. Very few Asians or black people were in this borough. During the weekend, some Asians or African people would visit Westminster.

In Piccadilly, there were a couple of Indian restaurants and the owners were from Moulvibazar, Sylhet. Another ward, mostly with Bengali people, was in Piccadilly. There were about 15-16 restaurants in Piccadilly.

Ms Hilda Griffith: I mean obviously on the estate we have the community centre and I believe a lot of them use that and you know, I suppose, their interaction is gradually growing the longer they are here, and they will become more accustomed to everything that is going on around the area.

Helping one another

Haji Arob Ali: Sometimes, I have sought help from others who can understand better English. For important issues, I would take someone with me so it was OK.

Bengali neighbours would help me, but I'd rarely seek help from English neighbours. Mostly from our own community people. Some people were educated in the Bengali community and they helped.

Alhaj Uster Ali: There was quite a bit, at that time there were about 30-40 families. I had connections with all the Bengali families because I used to help them out a lot. I knew all about this country, I had already lived here for 15 years. I had already helped many families, so I was quite experienced.

Yes, I used to work in Paddington during the night so I was free during the day. Once I came back from work, there was a local Bengali man crying on my door step. I asked him why he was crying, he replied to me 'My flight is at three, I don't know how to get there and that will mean my paid ticket will be wasted'.

I replied to him that I just came back from a night shift and you're crying at my door, could you not find any other Bengali? So I told him to come; I grabbed his bags and took him to get an emergency medical, and then I dropped him off for his flight. Since then, he has passed away but his children told me that he used to tell them how much I helped him.

We used to write letters every Saturday and Sunday. Some people could not write, so I would go round and write for them. I used to help some people who needed it because we also wanted to know what was happening back home.

We used to write on the weekends because we had full time jobs. I used to work in the holidays for double pay. I used to work for seven weeks then go back home.

Mrs Harisun Nessa: When my husband came back from Bangladesh, he knew and learnt of Bengalis in the area. From there we met an elderly lady who we stayed with and who was very helpful and treated me like her daughter. My kids were troublesome and would make a mess everywhere, even on her bed! She was very sweet and would assure me that it was ok and I would clean their mess. She and her husband have passed now but she helped me a lot and would let me pray in her room as there was no space in my room.

Mrs Harisun Nessa: We met an elderly man who migrated from Bangladesh who would visit us on a daily basis. He would tell me that his day would only be complete when he saw us. He was alone in this country. He used to sell garment's to the local neighbours, these garment's were from Bangladesh. He would keep these supplies in our house.

Alhaj Md Abdun Noor: At that time we would help each other. Whenever we would receive a letter from our country, the rest of us would ask about the contents of the letter. In the letter, our relatives normally asked for money to buy land or build a house or anything else. When someone wouldn't have enough money to send, everyone would offer loans.

Mr Abdul Moobin: In the Bengali community people always come to me with their letters and other things to get help with. I always read their letters for them and write replies to their family members, as they were not able to read or write Bengali.

Ms Noorjahan Begum: When we were in a hotel we came across a Bengali family, who helped us during that time. We did not know about social security, so they made phone calls for us and sent us a form and asked us to go to the office to get financial support. At the beginning we were using our own money.

Mr Joe Hegarty: We tended to work through Mr Chowdhury, the forerunners of the Marylebone Bangladesh Society. Bangladeshi people tended to go to them and they tended to come to us. Mr Chowdhury was very good.

He worked on London Transport, at one of the stations. His English was good so that was a factor because a lot of people's English was not very good, so they weren't confident about coming to see people like me.

And, of course, Murad Qureshi's father (Mushtaq) used to be around at that time, although he didn't live in this area, he lived just next door in Little Venice. He was very prominent in this area so those were people we tended to meet and deal with.

Mr Guthrie McKie: Different groups set up and the one in my area is the Queen's Park Bangladeshi Association. There's one here and there's one in South Westminster. I'm not sure... often they perpetuated the problem because often their audience was the first generation Bangladeshis who understandably wanted their way of the world reinforced.

I can understand why people wanted to do that – to go into a room where everyone spoke the same language as you and ate the same food as you. I think they could have done more and they should have done more.

I'm disappointed in the Bangladeshi groups; I don't they're doing enough to draw the Bangladeshi community into an understanding of what it is to live in a more open society.

Chapter six

Views of some non-Bengalis

Bangladeshis talked about bringing some of their culture and traditions with them, so we wondered what that may have been like for the non-Bangladeshi population in Westminster. Below are some of the stories told by professionals who worked in Westminster during the 70s.

Mr Joe Hegarty: We used to get invited to a range of things, like Eid celebrations with orange juice, which was unusual for those of us who were used to alcohol. I found myself being introduced to people not from the area, because people of relative distinction in the Bengali community from all over London would be bought to these things. They were the more articulate, able, entrepreneurial people you met, rather than the ordinary average people.

Over time, these things change and people get more confident and the children grow up and they speak perfect

English. I remember when I used to go round on the doorsteps, it would be the children who would interpret.

Most of the fathers were working, in restaurants, hotels, rag trade, London transport, but it was in the 80s when jobs started to dry up that people weren't in work. But at first most people were working.

Of course, over a period the produce in the market started to change, it took a long time actually. One of the noticeable things was that the traders were white and a lot of the customers were from minority communities.

The traders were for a long time quite racist in their views, and there may even still be elements of that around, but it's much less because there are traders of all sorts of different backgrounds, and all sorts of people go to them and buy all sorts of produce.

One of the things we found in the Bangladeshi community is the very high respect for elders, and that doesn't really convey into the British culture, as you may know.

Therefore, older Asian people were not treated how they were used to. They weren't treated any differently to people from a white background, but white people probably wouldn't have expected it to the same extent.

Mr Guthrie McKie: To give an example, there's a youth club in my ward, it's part of the London Tigers. It's a Muslim boys' club, or something like that. A few years ago they asked for funding and we said we'd fund a youth club for boys and girls, but not just a boy's youth club. They wouldn't, so we said we're not going to give you money to perpetuate separation between boys and girls. It's that sort of thing that I'd like to see more of. I'd like to see them challenging some of these things.

Dr Andrew Elder: I became a GP in 1972 and I joined a training practice at the bottom end of Lisson Grove. That was my first year and I stayed on in the same practice as a partner and I worked continuously in that area right up until my retirement, which was in 2008.

During that time we started in a small shop at the bottom end of Lisson Grove, just one room, then we moved to a flat on the Lisson Green Estate, then to the Lisson Grove Health Centre, and finally to Paddington Green Health Centre in 1999.

When do you recall first coming across the Bengali community?

Well, maybe I did earlier, but my first clear memory is of a family who moved in probably the mid-70s. So just one or two families arriving in the Lisson Green area, well, the newly-built Lisson Green Estate. I remember one family wanting to make contact with us as a local doctor, and inviting two or three of us, who were partners, and a social worker, to lunch - which was an invitation we were very pleased to accept.

It was in the spirit of an opportunity for us to meet a Bengali family and learn a bit about Bengali life, but also just to meet as people really. And I'm sure for them to begin to make contact and understand the local practices, so I have a clear a memory of that. So I would think in the mid-70s is when Bengali families started to move in. They all came from Sylhet I think, I seem to remember learning that.

What sort of things did they come to you for help with? Was it just health or wider than that?

I'm sure it was wider than that because the approach we had to being a GP was that although health is the main concern that somebody comes to see a doctor for, there are always other things that are associated with health. There are always worries, there are always family dimensions, and certainly for a community that is settling in a new country there are going to be lots of concerns about that as well - missing home, how you are received in a new community, language problems, maybe different attitudes to health and living.

Chapter seven

Support services in Westminster

We spoke with interviewees about services or organisations that supported people as they adjusted to Westminster. We found that people often integrated through their children's schools. Education was a priority and parents were encouraged to communicate with non-Bangladeshis through them. Schools tended to be receptive and accommodating to migrants of all backgrounds.

We have also included the stories of some of the other professionals who were involved with this population at the time.

School

Alhaj Md Abdun Noor: My eldest son was almost grown up when he came to this country, but I sent him to language school. The rest of them went to school. School was just opposite my building so they went by themselves. The teachers were very good; I met them on many occasions. They normally called me to have a meeting for my children. They called parents in to report on the progress of their children.

Mrs Anowara Begum: The first time I took my daughter to nursery I received a good welcome from school. The teachers were fantastic, even other parents, white or black, everyone was so lovely.

Haji Fazar Ali: My eldest child went to secondary school whilst my other three children went to Gateway Primary School. The teachers used to care for everyone.

Mr Fazal Miah: One of my children was born in Bangladesh and one was born here. One of my neighbours was Sri Lankan, who helped take my wife to hospital. The doctors and nurses were amazing, big differences to now. Previously they were lovely. The behaviour of doctors and nurses of that time and current time is a day and night difference.

Mrs Hosne Ara Moobin: I still remember when I first dropped off my son, he wouldn't eat during lunch time. The headmistress once called me in and reported that my son was not eating anything during lunch time. If he does not eat how can he learn? I was surprised to see that during lunch time she would take him to her room and eat her lunch and ask my son to eat with her. I could not forget her thoughtfulness.

Mr Abdul Hannan: My wife took my kids to school and everyone there was very nice and helped a lot. The schools were helpful as they used to take my kids out.

Mr Hifzur Rahman: When I was going to school in Bangladesh, my dad was in London, so he could not take me to school. So, I felt very excited to take my children to school. My eldest child failed his GCSEs. I did not put any pressure on him.

I told him he would not be able to have a good life if he does not do well in his education. Then, he put effort into his education and did a BTEC national and did a degree in design construction, which I was proud of. Now he has a good job and is in a good position in life.

Mr Abdul Moobin: I can't recall but probably I did. The teachers and staff were very helpful. There were no Bengali children in the school so I never met any Bengali parents.

Alhaj Muhib Uddin: The school was so helpful, and the health centres sent us a midwife to help us take care of our son, and advised us about the right milk and so on.

Alhaj Uster Ali: No, my daughter went to a school next to my work. I was not worried because I could drop them off and pick them up. The teachers were great because they would feed them milk and food.

Ms Azizun Khatun: The first time my husband took me to the doctor's and my parents-in-law also helped me. After the birth of my children I had to take them to clinics or other appointments.

I got encouragement from the clinics as well to learn English. They persuaded me and said because I had basic education it would be easier for me to learn English quickly. I took my child to nursery with my neighbour's child so it was OK. I was little bit worried as it was the first time they were going to school.

I always went to parents' meetings. I'd even arrange special meetings with their teachers and carefully look through their attendance and their progress. I checked their progress in every subject.

Alhaj Lala Miah: Gateway Primary School is an old school, when I sent two of my children there, they happily welcomed them. We received enough support from the teachers. They taught our children very carefully. I felt proud to say that all of my children become educated and got involved in banking or businesses.

Haji Arob Ali: Yes, I was very welcomed by the teachers. First couple of days I dropped my children off and later on they would go by themselves.

Mrs Hosne Ara Moobin: Neighbours were helpful whenever I'd ask for any help. One of the Irish families was very friendly, sometimes they'd visit us and we would also visit them. Their daughter and my daughter were friends. They always cared for us.

Mr Kobir Miah: At first it was a little difficult but when I went to school, it got easier. Within three months, I picked up the language. To communicate and get around wasn't an issue because there were some Pakistani brothers around.

There were very few Bengalis around, it was two of us brothers in a class. In that school it was only two of us Bengali brothers, although there was no issue with communication because we had a Pakistani teacher named Sir Yaqub, who taught us how to conduct ourselves and communicate, and we also had an English teacher called Mrs Bartason, she was very good, I still remember her today.

I took my child to the school. The teachers and the receptionist were very friendly.

Alhaj Abdur Rahman: Not really, in the beginning it was not known to me, there were no Bengali organisations or anyone to give us some advice or direction. We did not receive any advice from anywhere about how to register with the Labour Office. The only advice I got was that although I had no children in Bangladesh yet, I should say I had children.

Mr Khalil Miah: Children in this country were nice, I had no fears. My children went to Gateway. Sometimes I picked my children up from school and sometimes my wife used to pick them up. Gateway was very safe. I never, ever had any problems, nor did my children get into any trouble. The reason I didn't fear was because I know I raised my children right. Children only become naughty when they have no guidance, and we gave our children guidance.

Local people and services

Dr Andrew Elder: The Asian Families Project was the first of its kind in the country. One of the things we always felt was that Bengali patients would talk more about problems with their bodies, rather than addressing possible mental health problems. Somebody might come in and say I'm suffering from too much pain, or pain all over.

We had to learn not just to look for a physical cause of that pain, but to look more widely about possible psychological and social pressures that might be leading to it. But even if you do that, it might be quite difficult for a Bengali woman to speak openly about some of her worries to a western white male doctor. We had to think about all of those things – women were very important.

I can remember, as we got to know people, some quite good levels of trust developing. I can remember a family where people who were visiting from Bangladesh would be bought in to see me because I had become a reasonably known or trusted figure in the family.

So I remember seeing people's aunts or mothers and then they went away for two years and you saw them again. That could be quite frustrating and quite annoying in a way, because you have quite a busy life and suddenly you're being asked to see somebody because they're taking the opportunity to have a bit of a check-up. They would come as temporary residents, but to a certain extent it was ok. I can remember some quite serious illnesses.

Somebody's mother arrived one day - I think she had only been in the country two days - with very advanced cancer of the hand. She then stayed with the family and became very seriously ill about two years after we had arranged immediate treatment for her. I do have a memory of going just when she was dying. I remember going with a young doctor to visit her right at the end of her life. All the women were in one room and around her, where she was dying or had died.

Would that be likely? Complete gender segregation. We did what was needed. I also remember people sending the bodies of people home, presumably to be buried in Bangladesh. I remember that happening two or three times, maybe more.

Haji Surok Meah: During that time Westminster was not

as crowded as it is now. People were very nice and helpful. They seemed to be very fond of our people. For example, my neighbour was an old lady. Once a boy was murdered in Edgware Road, and this lady became very worried, she thought about me and asked my uncle 'Where is your boy?' She even waited for me until 5.45pm. When I finally arrived home she saw me and was so relieved.

Mrs Harisun Nessa: It was very nice back then. The English women would approach me and speak to me whenever I'd walk down the streets. They were a lot friendlier back then. They used to tell me how lucky I was, because I had twins (a boy and a girl).

Mrs Hosne Ara Moobin: We were living in Gloucester Terrace, a beautiful place, very clean, there were parks nearby, and everything was very pleasant. Shopkeepers and other service providers were very polite, especially when I responded politely. English people would help me in many ways.

Alhaj Md Abdun Noor: I did not have that much communication or interaction with the neighbours, but they always said hello or hi whenever we saw each other.

Mrs Anowara Begum: I used to get lost on the way to school but would always receive help from others. A funny story is when one day my husband asked me to collect his clothes from the laundry, which was only on the ground floor of the building.

I went to collect his clothes but couldn't work out where the laundry was. Then I showed the ticket to a white lady who helped me. She went with me inside the shop and collected the clothes for me.

Yes, I had some friends, Mrs Chowdhury, Hassan's

mum, and one white lady's name was Mary. Mary did a lot for me. Our next door neighbours were very helpful.

She had one child, whereas I had three, and we were all in one room with the children. She always took my children to her flat and allowed them to play with her child.

Mr Mohammed Siraj: All sorts of problems. Instead of just being a pharmacist, to them I was a social worker as well. They used to come to me with all sorts of problems.

Because they could communicate with you?

Because they could communicate with me.

What sort of problems?

Any kind of help. From immigration, personal problems, even if they wanted to borrow some money they would come to me as well.

What did you say to them?

I would sometimes lend them money.

And if they came with immigration problems or something like that, where did you send them? What did you do?

To the right appropriate places.

Mr Mohammed Siraj: One of the agendas was to help wherever I could with this community, because they will not get a job anywhere else. Most of the time, this was their first job. Not really. I was quite open minded. I helped them. I trained them. So no problems.

Mrs Harisun Nessa: My husband spoke English well and

was aware of the local services we were eligible for. A social worker used to help me with my 3 kids. She would come by for 2-3 hours and teach me how to read and write and taught me how to count to 100. She came for 3 months. We used to converse a lot and that was very helpful.

Mr Khalil Miah: My neighbour was an Irish lady, her name was Margaret, and she was a good friend. She was a very nice lady and she used to really take care of my wife and me also. She lived next door to us, we were number seven and she was number eight.

I used to work full time so she used to always tell me and my wife 'If you need any help or have any problems, call me', and slowly we became really close. There was never a problem, the area was nice. Margaret used to take my wife out sometimes, but also my wife used to go out by herself.

Mr Joe Hegarty: There was an organisation called the Community House Information Centre, which worked very closely with the community, including Bengali families, and they were very good at navigating the system. They would bring in people who could translate as well, which was a great help.

Talking about navigating the system, it's difficult enough if you're perfectly good at English, because the system was and is complicated, to get this benefit or that benefit. If your English is poor, it's twice as difficult, and they really needed an advocate. There were people who would come to us about benefits and we would take those interviews up with the DHSS (Department of Health and Social Services), as it was then.

Gradually as people became more confident, we held surgeries and people came to us with their issues and problems. The biggest one I can recall was housing, and the size of the houses, because they were large families.

It was very difficult to get housing of the appropriate size, even in places like Lisson Green, which had been built fairly generously by former standards. By various devices, like combining properties or allowing families to rent two properties, the council were able to help a bit in those circumstances.

One of the issues has been in the cooking of ghee and stuff like that, which is terribly bad for you. The life expectancy has been lower in Church Street than in the rest of Westminster. I remember we did manage to employ a young Bengali woman as a dietician, and that really helped. The health outcomes for Bangladeshi people are not anywhere near what they need to be.

Mrs Harisun Nessa: I used to send my middle to child to a play centre. I'd drop him off in the morning and pick him up at midday. I would pay 5p for those services. Once I would drop him off, I would then drop my elder daughter to school. There was a time when I would pay a lady to drop my elder daughter to school. She would then pick my daughter up and drop her home.

Alhaj Abdur Rahman: When I first came I went to Daventry Street, Westminster. We landed on October 30, 1963, along with two others, and got to Daventry Street by taxi at about 2am. I only had £5 in my pocket. There was a Bengali person, whom we were supposed to meet, but when we knocked on the door, he did not open.

Our taxi driver said that we better go to the nearest train station, rest there for the night, and then return early in the morning. Marylebone Station was closest; so he parked his taxi on a side road and walked with us to show us where it was. As we had no money we were not able to pay, but it was not a problem. He left us in the station and said he would come back in the morning.

In the morning at 7am we again went to Daventry Street and knocked on the door. They opened the door and gave us tea. The taxi driver also came to collect his money. He was a very good man, twice during the night he came to see us in the station to make sure that we were not lost. He was English.

Mr Abdul Hannan: I went back to Bangladesh and had my first son and came back to London in 1984. When my second child was born, in Middlesex Hospital, the experienced nurse took care of my wife as I was not happy with there being a male in the room.

Haji Fazar Ali: I got a lot of support from the health centres. In Marylebone, the health centres were very helpful.

Mr Abdul Sobur: There was an Indian doctor whom I could go to and speak with, and who many people spoke with. There were a lot of fights, yes, but also there were people who supported us a lot too.

Nowadays if you get lost, for example, and ask the police how to get to your destination, they will tell you without thinking twice. However, in those days, I hardly knew any English, and when I asked a policeman with the little English I did know they would not understand properly, nor would I understand them properly.

It was hard to communicate, but we always carried the addresses with us, so I showed him which address and instead of giving me directions he took me in his car to the doorstep of where I needed to go, to ensure I got there safely. This is how they helped us. There were always people who were good and who were bad. There was a type of people who were called skinheads, with shaved heads, who would beat people up and hurt them.

Ms Syeda Chowdhury: My manager was white, but used to tell me where to go and eat and used to show me what was halal and what wasn't halal, although majority of foods were not halal. They know me because of my husband too. After two months I became pregnant, and my daughter Jusna was born.

I used to go with an English lady who was my neighbour, she was Italian and I used to always give her curry from the restaurant, and because I didn't have a washing machine she said to give my washing to her and she'd do it for me. In Bangladesh all the women did the washing so I didn't really know or learn how to do it. So it was difficult for me. So I used to tell my husband to give rice and curry so the lady would wash our clothes.

Haji Fazar Ali: It was an amazing experience. At last I have to leave the hospital; they were so nice and kind and even though I was fine, they still did not want me to leave the hospital. I was not aware of the types of clothes that I needed to buy for the baby.

Lucie brought most of the important things but when I left hospital my luggage was full with free stuff from companies. Approximately 10-12 days I was in hospital, during which time they cared for me. Though I was not able to speak yet, they made every effort to help and support me. They provided fantastic services.

Mr Fazal Miah: Neighbours were very good, previously almost all people were helpful, I never faced any hostility from my neighbours.

Mrs Hosne Ara Moobin: Yes, I went to the Bangladesh centre on many occasions. They organised various cultural events.

My first child was born in St Mary's Hospital. I really appreciated their services. Fantastic services, the nurses and midwife frequently visited our house and taught me many things about baby caring. Services were so good that I can't even tell you, there is not a single thing that I can complain about against them.

Alhaj Lala Miah: During that time everything was very easy, people were helpful. I had no issue that I had to go to any agencies for any help. I dealt with any problem directly with the offices, even when my family joined me I applied to Westminster Council for accommodation and within a week they called me.

Lisson Grove Health Centre was very old; I first joined with them when my family arrived in this country. I had a doctor friend on Harley Street, his name was Peter. He was a consultant of Brompton Hospital; this gentleman helped me a lot. First he took my family to his hospital and checked on them there.

No there were no organisations as far as I know, I did not contact anyone. The school always contacted me for my children and I personally dealt with any issues such as absences. They would contact me over the telephone or send a letter.

Alhaj Muhib Uddin: The police were so helpful, they saw us lost and saw the address I wanted to go to written on my piece of paper, and ordered me a cab and explained to the cab driver for me where we wanted to go. They would try and communicate with me and be very welcoming.

Were your neighbours helpful? Anyone else?

They were very helpful, especially in the Easter

holidays, they used to invite me over for tea and cakes, which helped build a better relationship and helped me learn more English.

I had my first child in the UK. My wife had a very difficult pregnancy and had to stay in the hospital for one month. Then after two months she had to make regular visits and the nurse would come to our house to check on her. The hospital staff were so nice and caring. When the baby was born the nurse came over to me saying, Mr Uddin, you have a very nice baby! They were really nice and would tell me to bring my baby regularly to check his weight, as he was premature.

Mrs Hosne Ara Moobin: I never went for any help from any agencies. I tried to do things myself and if I could not do anything my husband was there. Of course he was quite busy with his job, but whenever it was necessary he took time off.

Ms Azizun Khatun: It was amazing. They helped me to bath and dry my hair. All of them were so fond of my hair. I was cared for a lot in hospitals. After giving birth I had to stay in hospital at least 10 days.

Mr Kobir Miah: No not at all, but at the same time we did not go to seek them out, we didn't really need the help of local agencies.

Alhaj Uster Ali: I used to live less than 500 yards from the hospital. I used to live in Praed Street so I always used to go down. The nurses were great. They took care of us when the twins were born.

Haji Fazar Ali: They were helpful. My white neighbours

weren't as helpful as Bengali neighbours, but if you needed help you could still ask them.

One day I was coming back from school. I was meant to get off the bus at Piccadilly Circus but instead I got off the bus at Green Park. It was dark and I did not know what to do. My dad gave me a card with my address and said if I ever got lost, show someone the card. I found a lady and showed her the card and she took me home.

Ms Noorjahan Begum: I had some problems sending my children off to school, I needed help from others. There was a voluntary organisation in Church Street area called 'CHIC'. They'd run English classes. I went there and found another Bengali woman also attending this class. I did six weeks of classes there on English, and at the same time I also motivated some others to enrol. Six weeks later I went to a job at the Bayswater Embassy Hotel. I'd only have to say either 'yes' or 'no'. I needed a job to help with household costs.

Haji Surok Meah: There was a Bengali doctor, most of the Bengalis would go to him, but I didn't. I thought that I could communicate in English, so I felt comfortable with seeing an English doctor, so I went to an English doctor in Chapel Street. I was healthy, so I didn't need to go to the doctor's often.

Alhaj Uster Ali: This country was okay. When my wife first came we had social workers who taught her how to manage in this country.

Edgware Road, North of the Junction of Harrow Road, 1963

Images © Westminster City Archives

Baker Street, New Lighting, 1963

Accident prevention hoarding opposite 204-5 Edgware road, 1960

Images © Westminster City Archives

Images © Westminster City Archives

Demolition of property in Edgware Road, 1962

Flooding outside 395-97 Edgware road caused by a burst water main, 1910

Images © Westminster City Archives

Church Street Market, looking towards Lisson Grove, 1965

Chapter eight

Leisure time

We asked the Bangladeshi migrants about what they did in their spare time and found they valued socialising. They had a variety of hobbies and interests but some struggled to find spare time.

With friends

Alhaj Lala Miah: Before bringing our family over, we were single, so we would contact each other from one restaurant to another and meet at a place, and go to a park or a restaurant in Brick Lane together. We also watched Indian films as there were no Bengali films available in London. There was a cinema in Tolmer Square, near Euston Station (it's gone now), and we'd watch films there or at another cinema in Brick Lane.

Mr Abdul Hannan: There was Green Park and Hyde Park close by, where English people would play football. Even though I could not speak English they would involve me and teach me how to play. People were very friendly.

They did not really have much when I was there. However, I did go to one music event after I finished work.

Mr Hifzur Rahman: I stayed a lot in Brighton. If the weather was good I would go to the seaside.

Haji Fazar Ali: With my friends I used to go to the cinema.

Alhaj Muhib Uddin: I used to go to music concerts, but do not remember what they were called.

Mr Kobir Miah: I used to travel from one town to another on my weekends.

Mr Abdul Moobin: At that time I was not very pious, but I attended Bangladeshi conferences or concerts whenever I heard of them and was able to manage.

Alhaj Abdur Rahman: I had very little time spare time to enjoy; I was the only member of my family, so I had to look after all of them, so I was eager to earn more money. I was the third son of my parents, two of my elder brothers were married but they were not in employment.

Every year I bought some land and they used to cultivate those lands. However, their life was better than me as they had nothing to be worried about.

Alhaj Abdur Rahman: I didn't have much free time, but whenever I got time I normally went to Hyde Park, Speakers' Corner. People gave political speeches so I spent two or three hours listening to them. It was the only thing I enjoyed during that time.

So whenever I would have some free time I would go there. Good to be there and at the same time it was an opportunity to learn something. On Sundays, when I would have a full day off, I also visited Barrister Abbas Ali. I had a very good relationship with him. I did bits and pieces with him as well. He always advised me to be involved in education, but I could not follow his advice.

Haji Arob Ali: Normal days off were on Saturdays and Sundays, mostly on Sundays as we went to the cinema or met people somewhere, and at night we'd cook together. At that time we barely watched TV. To save money, the owner did not allow watching TV all the time. Economic thinking was predominant during that time.

Occasionally music events were organised in Aldgate, and people participated. I was young during that time and took part. People also played cards then.

Mr Khalil Miah: Our parents and uncles were at work so we had fun. We went clubbing (giggles). There was a club in Piccadilly called Mecca where mostly the young generation went. All the young Bengalis, Chinese and Africans went.

Mr Abdul Sobur: During that time we enjoyed ourselves and had fun, although there used to be fights with our people.

With family

Ms Azizun Khatun: Mostly I enjoyed time with my children. Whenever I had an appointment at the clinic I would take my children and go a bit earlier and spend some time with other parents.

Haji Fazar Ali: I did not take them to any Christmas or street parties. I used to take them to mosque sometimes.

Mr Khalil Miah: I used to look after my kids, on my days off I used to take my children to the park and play with them. I also enrolled both my sons into karate.

Mrs Harisun Nessa: I once took my kids to the park and my middle son once ran straight in to the pond! My husband had to chase after him and drag him out!

Chapter nine

Women's stories

As their husbands tended to work away, women were often left to run the home. This meant that they were in charge of caring for the children and had greater interaction with the communities in which they lived.

Most of the interviewees reported that they were able to integrate well and that they got along with people of all backgrounds, however, some also reported being affected by the tensions rife in that period. Those that worked did so in a range of jobs, but sewing was common amongst women.

Role at home

Mrs Hosne Ara Moobin: There were three or four families in Baker Street. One of them was Mrs Reba's family. I mostly visited them, almost every week, as our children had grown up together so we met every single time. We also visited important places with the children.

Mr Abdul Moobin: My first child was born in St Mary's Hospital, my wife mostly dealt with the doctors and nurses as I had to go to work. But the doctors and nurses were fine. When she gave birth I was not beside her, I saw my child in the evening but the doctors and nurses were very helpful.

Ms Syeda Chowdhury: So one of my children was born in 1971, then another was born in 1973, and then another one in 1974. So they were all really young so it was hard for me. For example, changing nappies alone because I hardly had any support. I used to say to myself, when will I be able to sleep, because it was hard to sleep during the night with the children, so I said to God, when will you make my children older so that I can sleep throughout the day!

Mr Mohammed Siraj: Men were the bread winners so they used to be out. Women were looking after the kids and they literally ran the homes. So I used to see more women rather than men because they would come to the shop with their prescriptions or buy food or milk for the babies. Again the language was a major problem. Hardly anyone could speak English at the time.

Mrs Harisun Nessa: I didn't know people for me to enjoy myself or for me to go out with. I didn't have a TV either. My daily routine would consist of looking after the kids, dropping them to school, cooking, cleaning and taking them to the parks when I had a chance.

Integrating into society

Mrs Syeda Chowdhury: In 1985 I went to language classes at North Westminster School. At that time mostly white and black people were here. I even went to the Harrow Road to an English language class. It was not easy for me as my children were very small, one of my sons was two and another one was younger than him. My husband took time off on my class time. I left one with him and one of them was always with me.

Ms Syeda Chowdhury: In terms of ladies, I was the only one. Then a student of my father's had come to the country so I went to see him, I used to call him uncle due to the fact that he was a friend.

Everyone used to look after and care for me there though. When my husband used to come he used to eat in the restaurant with me, but because I was alone a lot of the time I used to come back up to the flat and I used to cry a lot because I had no one and hardly had anything to do. I used to get frequent headaches too. When I went to the doctor's, the doctor would say that this was because I was upset with my current situation.

No, no one made any comments like that. In fact, people used to help me when I used to go to the shop because I used to go to the shop on my own. Because my husband used to work, I was responsible for getting the babies' food and nappies. People used to see me and take care of me and understand that I would require help.

Ms Azizun Khatun: First couple months I never really left the house, but when I started having children, I began to go outside and see the area properly.

Ms Noorjahan Begum: I had no problem with interacting with white people. Since I started my job, I have had to work with mostly white people.

Mrs Hosne Ara Moobi: Feeling was very good, people were very nice and neighbours were cooperative. Whenever I went to the shops or anywhere else everyone was nice and received me very well. Only thing was that I missed my family members, relatives and friends.

Alhaj Abdur Rahman: No, I had loads of friends from other backgrounds, not just Bengali. I was a little bit fearful of black people. Whenever I saw someone unknown I never walked past them, I would have crossed the road to avoid them. The situation was not like today; when we were in need, there was no one else around.

But in East London it was different. In 1970 they faced troubles and fought together, they had grouped together and would stand up to anything together. Most of the people in this area were in hotels and catering jobs. But in East London, people were working in tailoring and leather factories.

Mr Joe Hegarty: When we found out there were tensions between individuals, we didn't want to get involved. People had different views on things because there was the traditional Bengali view on things, where the elders were the people who represented the community, and no women. And there were others who were more progressive.

I remember a bit later, two women coming along to the surgery, by this stage we had got past it all being channelled through one person, and saying to me 'Those old men don't speak for us! Be careful of speaking to them because they're not representative of our view.' Of course, the men had been here for a while. They had to some extent assimilated and quite a lot of them did speak some English and knew their whereabouts. Whereas the women would not speak English, but I do remember there were classes for women to learn English, so it became one of the things that did happen.

Mr Guthrie McKie: I think they've needed the same support as anybody else from a low income, and I think the biggest problem in the Bengali community is the fact that the first generation women tended not to speak English and were often not literate.

That's a big drawback for them and it's a drawback for talk about engagement with the wider community. It's not a drawback for their children, of course, because their children have been educated, they speak English. But the sense of isolation of older Bengali women in the community is quite significant. I think it's probably too late now to go through an education process with them, now they're in their 60s and 70s. I think the people that should have addressed it should have been the Bengali community, but they didn't. And I'm not saying because back home they didn't, they didn't have to do it. And I think there was a responsibility for Bengali men to do something and they didn't. I think if you get that resistance from the families, from the elder members of the family, it's difficult for the wider non-Bangladeshi community to try and influence that.

Alhaj Uster Ali: Life is hard, for normal people life is hard. But my wife dealt with it well. It was a little hard, we lived in a small room because we did not take the house provided by the railway service. My kids wanted to stay in Edgware Road.

> *We asked the local GP if children would come to him without their parents?*

Dr Andrew Elder: I remember emerging problems for young women, to do with their privacy growing up. Maybe they had a boyfriend? Maybe they were considering using contraception? These things couldn't be dealt with openly with the family.

They did, that's right. And then trying to, as a doctor, decide how much it was reasonable to hold that confidentially, but also encouraging them to try and be a bit more open. But that could be very, very difficult. Provided the young woman was of a reasonable age then the confidentiality was fine, and one would reassure her of that. But you might explore with her what were the barriers to being a bit more open.

Employment

> *It is often assumed that Bengali women who had settled in the 70s were not in paid employment and were more likely to be homemakers. Although their roles as mother, wife, daughter and daughter-in-law seemed to be a priority for them, we are delighted to have found Bengali women who have broken that stereotype.*

Mr Mohammed Siraj: They normally worked in restaurants initially, but when their kids started growing up they started applying to different places. I can remember in 19... I can't remember the exact year. Very early on, a Bengali girl came to me and applied for a job. She was wearing a hijab. In the 70s this was very rare, and she said 'Do you mind?', and at that time there were a lot more English customers. She thought they might object, but I said 'No, not to me, it doesn't matter', and I employed her.

She could speak English?

She could speak English. She was born here and brought up here.

Mr Guthrie McKie: Well, most of the Bengali women, like many other communities, didn't work in the first generation. They took a very traditional housewife role.

Dr Andrew Elder: There was a lot for us to learn about really. It was certainly a challenging process for us in the first place, but there were also a lot of people, maybe this is a little later, in the Bengali community who helped.

We had a wonderful Bengali health advocate. She was an enormous help to us. She used to accompany families in to see us, to interpret but more importantly to help us understand something about family life and family culture and to explain how perhaps to get the best out of a doctor.

She was an intermediary. She was a really, really important figure if you are looking at how families got on in relation to health things in Marylebone. She was around for many years. She was a very wise, very tactful woman, very committed to the Bengali community, but also was able to easily make friends with us and was a very good intermediary. She and some colleagues later went on to establish the Marlborough Family Service, a special Asian families project.

That project was really to try and help Bengali and

other Asian families with mental health problems, as it was easier for us to respond to physical health problems, because doctors are all trained in that way. To help at a mental health level, you have to understand culture and psychology and religious customs and all those other things which we wouldn't immediately know about. So there was this Asian family project to help with mental health problems.

Ms Khaleda Qureshi: I started sewing very early on in my London life, and I'm still continuing. Murad was a little baby. One day my husband took me to an Italian shop, as they were advertising for a sewing role. They showed me how to sew with this machine asked me to go for a trial.

I did sewing with my mum, so I managed to sew without any problems. The owner of the shop said that it was easy to recognise people who are skilled at sewing and that she was sure that I would be able to do the job. My first job was a pair of trousers. At that time to make a pair of trousers we would charge 14 shillings (roughly £10 in today's money).

Ms Syeda Chowdhury: Back then my husband went and talked to a cake factory near Charing Cross for me to have a job, and they agreed to give me a job. It wasn't that far from Sidcup, maybe about 10 or 12 stations. Back then I didn't know English very well. Because it was a factory I was told I had to work the early shift, and for around two months I continued to work there. Because I didn't know English very well I didn't understand much.

The cakes came in a box. I was told to add different things to the cakes, such as fruit and nuts. I was working with a lady who would finish this, which left me confused and without anything to do. Then the manager came and started counting the boxes on our sides and there are no boxes on my side because I couldn't find anything to do.

Then I thought to myself, how can a manager pay me if I am not doing anything?

The lady is not letting me do anything so how am I meant to complete the task? Then I went on my own accord to the manager to say there's something wrong, the lady keeps doing everything, the response I got to that was to let them continue because everyone will get the same pay anyway. The manager used to look after me too and used to check if I was eating and was feeling ok.

Me and my friend started work at the same time in the school. Mr Philip Allen was the head teacher.

My English was not that good, but the school wanted Bengali support staff there.

Chapter ten

Religion

For us, Islam and religion has always been a prominent part of our identity. Things like prayer and observing Ramadan are woven into our lives and encouraged through friends and family, and even on TV!

However, a common theme shared by early Bangladeshi migrants was that access to Islam was more limited. As a result, it became rare that people would fast during Ramadan or celebrate during Eid. Islamic principles have strengthened through the generations.

Religious practice

Mr Khalil Miah: I sent my daughter to an Islamic club where she learned how to pray and read the Quran.

Haji Surok Meah: Sometimes I could not observe prayer at the correct times due to my work commitments, but I never missed Ramadan in my life. I remember mostly fasting alone. I did my sehri (the meal consumed early in the morning, before fasting) with mango and carnation milk.

Alhaj Md Abdun Noor: People usually prayed at home, there were no mosques during that time. I had a lungee with me and sometimes I did my prayer with the lungee.

No we did not have any problem when performing namaaz. In the beginning, we were not that concerned with praying. I did not observe Ramadan at the beginning. Nobody knew when Ramadan started nor when it ended. However, our fathers tried to inform us of the dates in comparison to English months. Apart from that, it was not possible to observe Ramadan.

I never prayed in my workplace. I remember once I performed Eid prayer near Commercial Road, in the house of Haji Taslim Ali. I went there with some of my friends. It was not a mosque, it was his house, so many people were there so we squeezed in and perform Eid prayer.

A couple of Eids passed by in the beginning that I was not aware of. So after three or four Eids, some of my friends somehow got the information that the Eid Jamaat would be held in Haji Taslim Ali's house in East London. I went there with one of my friends, so this was my first Eid in this country.

Mrs Harisun Nessa: I would pray daily and the fasts were lengthy at the time as it took place during the summer. I used to take my kids to Hyde park to pass time; my kids would play whilst I would sit on a bench and fast. During those times men wouldn't really fast, your grandfather didn't fast! It was only me and another one of our family friends, we would break our fasts together. Our daily meals were rice and chicken, your grandfather would get food from Southall.

In those days we never knew when Eid was as we didn't have the means or the people to inform us. There were days when I would miss the second Eid as I didn't know when Eid was.

Ms Azizun Khatun: Women did not face any difficulties with practicing religion. During that time men did not usually practice religion either.

Mr Abdul Hannan: I did practice my religion freely and no one minded. In the room I stayed in with seven other people, praying was a struggle, due to the lack of space. I was very excited, I woke up and had a shower as though there was something to celebrate. However, all the men around me were going to work on Eid, so I did too. We did not celebrate Eid. I did not keep my fasts during Ramadan in those days.

Ms Khaleda Qureshi: No I did not find any difficulties to do my religious duties. This is a personal matter, there were no interruptions.

On first Eid day, in the beginning I was very upset, as it was not even easy to make contact with my relatives in Bangladesh. If you sent a letter it would take ages. Telephone communication was not as easily accessible.

At least one week before, you would have to notify the

operator that you were intending to call someone in your own country. Even the telephone conversation would not be cleared.

Haji Fazar Ali: I was young, so I did not pray much. You could not practice freely, but slowly it became easier to practice your religion in public. People were scared of the skinheads. I never missed Ramadan. It was easier in those days as I felt the days were shorter.

Mrs Hosne Ara Moobin: Regent's Park Mosque was the nearest mosque to us. On Eid day we went there with our children. There was no other mosque around this area except Regent's Park. Occasionally, on Fridays I went there but I never faced any difficulties.

Thanks to Allah, I performed my religious activities even in my work place. No one protested or distracted me. In fact, they supported me during my religious practice.

The big difference is that it's very lonely, even today I feel that the celebration of Eid is not like in our country. Because, on Eid day in our country, relatives or neighbours would visit in groups. They would do their salaams and eat the different foods, but things like that are not done here.

I still miss this part of celebration. Yes, nowadays sometimes some family members or relatives come to visit on Eid day, but that same excitement is not there.

Yes, I observed Ramadan from the beginning. Timing was the factor, long days, but I adjusted and accepted it, therefore it was OK.

Ms Azizun Khatun: First year I could not observe Ramadan, my mother-in-law asked me not to do this as the day was very long.

Alhaj Uster Ali: Before, we did not pray as much. There were not many mosques. We used to pray Tahajud (a late night prayer). People used to look after each other and support each other. When one child was bad the whole community knew.

Alhaj Uster Ali: At that time there was not a consistent mosque. I even led the prayer.

Mr Abdul Moobin: I used to practice in Bangladesh but it was difficult to do here, even in our own accommodation, as it was so congested. There was no bathroom either. The first Eid I did was in Regent's Park Mosque. I can't remember if I did any Eid before that.

No, during that time I did not fast. After the arrival of my wife in this country, I began to observe Ramadan. I was just fasting, not causing any problems for others, and neither did anyone else cause any problems for me.

Mr Kobir Miah: Yes, the first Eid we all bought food together, we went outside and ate together. We had a lot of fun. Once we became a little organised in this country and a mosque was built, we fasted and prayed.

Alhaj Lala Miah: No, whatever practice I did I had no problems, though of course I could not go to mosque, due to fear of personal safety in the street. I personally felt that I have full liberty to observe my religion, no one obstructing me. I freely did and until today doing the same.

I prayed at home, but there was very little chance to do this in my work place. Basically we would have to work until 1-2am, especially in the Indian restaurants.

The day and night difference was difficult, sometimes we didn't know when Eid or Shab-e-Baraat or Shab-e-Qadr was. There were no good communications - even amongst us. There were no telephones or television in every household. We had poor communication with each other. There was no Bengali newspaper either.

We could not attend any Eid prayer far away from us, we just attended the nearest Jamaat. We made good food when we joined our family, traditional pitas, or other food had been cooked and served.

Ms Noorjahan Begum: At that time not many people were fasting. Most of the people were openly smoking. It was not like now. Currently there is a strong Islamic trend everywhere but it was not before. There were not many places for prayer, Regent's Park Mosque was built after my arrival. Slowly people started to go to prayer.

Haji Arob Ali: There were no prayer facilities in Westminster, only on Eid day, we did our prayer in an open air field. Even Regent's Park Mosque was built later on. Most of us also went to Aldgate to perform Eid or Jumma prayer. Mostly people who wished to pray, they did it at home.

At that time we could not do the prayer during working hours and had very little time to go to mosque, so whatever we did do we did it at home. Not many of us practiced religion but those who wished to do so, did during their time off at home.

I remember, for my first Eid prayer I went to Aldgate. No facilities were in Westminster, even Regent's Park Mosque was not there.

Yes, I fasted during Ramadan. But the saree was very difficult for us. Sometimes we ate early and went to bed, or sometimes we waited for late at night. Occasionally, we fasted without having our saree. But it is true, many of us did not perform Ramadan.

Mr Fazal Miah: At that time not many people bothered about Eid. Few people went to Eid prayer, it was not like now. There were not many mosques around either.

Ms Syeda Chowdhury: Of course I kept my fasts. I know that I am a Muslim.

Mr Hifzur Rahman: No. Working at restaurants I would pray, if the restaurant was too busy then I would not pray on time. Overall, I could practice my religion freely.

There weren't many Eid Jamaats. The main one in London was the East London Mosque. My second Eid was at Brighton, in a park, there wasn't any mosque. The food was different to the food you eat on Eid day in Bangladesh. Slowly my dad taught me to cook.

I always fasted. I faced no difficulties with Ramadan. With sehri, me and my dad would wake up, eat, then sleep. When we had the restaurant, we could close up at midnight, then clean up the restaurant, then eat sehri, then go to bed.

Alhaj Muhib Uddin: I did not face any difficulties practicing my religion. We were very free to practice, the government did not stop us.

The first two years we were here we did not celebrate Eid at all. However, after that, in Seymour Place everyone would hire a hall together and do Eid prayer there. Then gradually we would do our five prayers in Regent's Park.

We could not really keep our fasts properly the first few years because it was really hard in that environment, especially working a lot, and there was not a large community of support. Until later, when mosques were built, like The East London Mosque, there were more Muslims which helped Ramadan awareness and give support.

Chapter eleven

Relationship with children

They were settling in a new country where the culture and living standards were very different to their own. As a result, we found stories of determination, whilst they spoke of nurturing their children between two very different cultures.

These parents showed great dedication to teaching their children about Bangladeshi culture and the Islamic way of life, whilst also prioritising their children's mainstream educational needs. Given that this generation of parents did not tend to practice Islam as frequently and were not as fluent in English, it was surprising to hear how much value they placed in instilling these values into their children.

We expected to hear stories of conflict and struggles. However, it seems that most parents shared a positive relationship with their British born children. Naturally we wondered if there may be a stigma attached to the idea of parents sharing difficult stories of raising their children between two very different cultures.

Mr Hifzur Rahman: I signed up to be the school governor, so I could understand the education system more clearly, which would help my children. Once my children went to Quintin Kynaston School, I was also the school governor. I took this position because the more I understood about education, the more I could help my children.

Alhaj Lala Miah: As parents we always dealt with them as a friend, that's why they shared everything with us, never hide anything. By having a good relationship we were able to help each other.

Mrs Anowara Begum: I always tried to raise my children to be well behaved and to have a proper education. I was not aware of the culture of this country so I always gave them time, helped them with their homework. I maintained a strict time table for them. I dropped them at school at the right time and at exactly 8pm it was their bed time. I still follow this same timetable.

Alhaj Muhib Uddin: I took them to nursery and dropped them off on the way to work. On the first day I was so happy, I got him up, gave him a bath, got him ready, had breakfast as a family, and then me and my wife both took him to nursery together.

I was never afraid, and usually I took them to school, or

my wife would take them. My main thought was that they would come home for lunch to eat.

Mr Joe Hegarty: The families tended to be together and you tended to have large extended families as well. I think that was a tremendous support to the children. I think that made it a bit different from the Afro-Caribbean community, having those networks. They helped a lot and were necessary in those days, stopping children getting into trouble. Because everybody was from the same area, people knew each other back then.

The teaching of religion

Ms Azizun Khatun - I will not allow my children to marry someone from a different religion, and I don't think any parent would agree to this.

Alhaj Md Abdun Noor: The main difficulty was to look after them, to check how they were behaving, have they been going to school and coming back home, have they been following their faith and culture? I tried my utmost to educate them on our religion and our language. Fortunately, three of my girls can read and write Bengali. They can speak Bengali very well.

Alhaj Md Abdun Noor: I am happy with what they have achieved, but I am completely happy with them as things are not quite what I expected. First of all, they have almost lost their religion, their language and their culture.

Alhaj Lala Miah: We never did any birthday parties at home, but they did in school. In terms of religious lessons, there were no good facilities at that time, but we got a private religious teacher to educate them on the Quran and namaaz. That much we were able to do.

Mr Fazal Miah: I gave them religious education. They read the Quran but not Bengali.

Alhaj Muhib Uddin: I got an Islamic teacher at home to teach them the Quran.

Education

Mr Joe Hegarty: I'll talk a bit about education. The children went to local schools and on the whole were very well behaved, compared to some of the other groups that were there. But for a long time they didn't achieve very highly, and obviously that was a bit of a concern.

I can't remember which way round it was, but either boys or girls, one gender did better than the other to begin with. We were worried about it but now, of course, both do perfectly well. One of the underlying issues was the way that girls were treated as second class. Now I think that situation has changed a lot.

But looking at education, for a long time children underachieved, and then began to achieve. It would be really interesting to find out why that was, but it may be because people struggled to integrate and understand the education system at that time. Certainly the families have always been aspiring as far as I can tell.

Chapter twelve

Preserving Bangladeshi culture

In the UK many people were concerned that there would be a loss of the Bengali identity and culture. They worried that their children would not speak the Bengali language and would adopt English culture. Many parents encouraged their children to speak Bengali at home and took their children on visits to Bangladesh, so that they could experience the Bengali culture and retain the language.

Nevertheless, despite parents' desires to retain the Bengali culture, many were also accepting of their children adopting parts of the English culture, as they realised that they would need to integrate with the society in which they lived.

Alhaj Md Abdun Noor: They are only Bengali because of their blood, their skin and their colour, but the rest of their identity is completely different. They lost their identity; they are neither Bengali nor English, something different.

There is a river near my house in Bangladesh. On the shore of the river there was a musi (shoemaker's) family. My father said that they have been residing there for more than 100 years, but they still had their own language. One of the boys of the family was my classmate. Once I went to their house. He called his sister to make a cup of tea for me. He used his own language and told her not to give the same cup that they had been using (presumably to provide me with a better cup).

They did not lose their language or identity, but my children lost their language and culture. That means my children are worse than the musi's children.

Mr Abdul Hannan: The biggest obstacle was that my children were adopting a British culture where they kept speaking in English and losing their Bengali culture. I supported their studies, but ensured that at home they only speak Bengali and were not allowed to speak English, so they would not forget.

Mr Mohammed Siraj: Their aspirations are, I think, to mingle with the community. This is their place.

So they came here to make money and send it back home?

Absolutely, that was the idea behind it, their home was Bangladesh, they never considered England as home. But now, the second generation are thinking more that this is their home, and Bangladesh is a holiday.

Alhaj Md Abdun Noor: My children came later, in 1987. During this time most of our family came to this country. But I was worried. My eldest son may go to college, but I just allowed him to learn some English and go for employment. My daughter went to primary school and then went to secondary school and completed her A levels.

She wished to go for further education but I did not allow her, as I was worried that she may damage the reputation of my family, she might lose our culture and family tradition. She was frustrated, she cried and even smashed some things at home, because she wanted to go for further education, but I was against this. After her marriage she obtained her degree.

Mr Abdul Hannan: I told my children they can associate with white children out of the house, but can never bring them home.

Ms Khaleda Qureshi: Two other Bengali parents were also sending their children to the same school. Mostly they played with English children. We were a little bit worried that the children may lose their culture and so, in 1970, we went back to Bangladesh. Our aim was to stay in Bangladesh for a period of time, so that they can learn about our culture first.

I kept up our culture inside of our home, and took care of them, but all affairs outside of the home were dealt with by my husband. I was little bit strong on them, but my husband asked me to allow them to move freely.

He said – if you don't allow them to do certain things by themselves, then you lose control of them. Just give them an awareness and an understanding of the outside environment.

Mr Fazal Miah: It's OK, praise to Allah, they are fine. They mostly speak English. I don't mind because they have to live in this culture.

Haji Arob Ali: I would not tell them they are British, they are Bengali and I tried my best to keep them Bengali. Although they have learnt English in school, at the same time we taught them Bengali, and Islamic religion as well.

Mr Hifzur Rahman: I had 100% commitment to maintaining our culture when raising my children. I taught them Bengali and Arabic.

I took my children to Bangladesh and also got them married in Bangladesh. My children were very good at socialising with people in Bangladesh, and I also gave them a tour of Bangladesh. In this way they came to love Bangladesh. My children attended Bengali class at the Marylebone Society, and I taught them Arabic at home.

Mr Abdul Hannan: My kids played with a lot of white children and I did not mind. This is because when they came home I got an Arabic and Bengali teacher to teach them so they did not forget their culture.

I did not want my children to forget their own culture, and I thought about sending my eldest either back to Bangladesh or to Islamic school. However, I did not get the chance, but ensured that they were taught our culture at home.

Alhaj Muhib Uddin: No, they will only be able to marry inside our culture, Bengali and Muslim. However, two of my children did not listen and married out of my culture, and I was not happy for some time. In the end, both my son's wives converted to the Islamic faith, which changed my perception and I accepted their marriages.

I ensured I told my children that at home they are not allowed to speak English, as I did not want them to forget their language. If they spoke in English, I would not respond to them. I let them play outside with their friends, but gave them a curfew, and they were not allowed home a minute late.

They are Bengali and must speak to me in Bengali, always.

Mr Abdul Moobin: We did not force anything, we left things open to them. We educated them about our faith and culture and it is up to them to do what they want to do.

Mrs Hosne Ara Moobin: To be honest, I never thought that my child would adopt a different culture, as I believed that it depended on me, depended on how I was raising them. I thought that if I give them the correct education about our culture and tradition, that they would not be influenced by others. But, it is true, I felt that, as they have been growing in a different culture, they will not be able to maintain 100% of their own culture.

I taught them about the good sides and bad sides of both cultures, and advised them to have the appropriate education. I also explained to them how we do our religious activities and celebrations. I never stopped them from taking part in other cultural activities, but emphasised that they should keep their own culture.

Mr Kobir Miah: Yes, my children took part in multiple events regardless of cultures, they went to birthday parties and functions, just not dances.

Chapter thirteen

The melting pot

In the parents' generation, those with little English were able to live in the developing Bengali community without requiring too much interaction with their English neighbours. However, as they became more settled, some became more invested in local concerns, with some Bengali representatives in the council.

The children were mostly allowed to integrate with children of other backgrounds, because parents understood that this was a part of their new environment. However, parents generally strongly disagreed with marrying non-Bengalis; the cultural differences caused parents to feel uncomfortable, although a few were resigned to the idea that they could not forbid their children from developing feelings for non-Bengali partners.

Relationships with local people

Ms Azizun Khatun: I had very little interaction with non-Bengalis. Later on my father-in-law sent me to an English class. I continued there for a period.

Mr Abdul Moobin: English neighbours were keeping their distance and this was not because of racial biases or for any other things, but because of our cultural and language differences.

Mr Kobir Miah: We had English neighbours who were very friendly, some of them had families with children my age and we would play, they were very friendly. Although there was one person who always stood out. On the road which I took to go to school there was a woman who would always say 'good boy, nice boy' to me. She used to say it every day and it used to make me very happy.

Ms Noorjahan Begum: Back then it was really very good. Very few people of our community were able to speak English during that time, but our neighbours were quite good and helpful. At that time, most of the English people were helpful, not like now. Currently, it is very hard to identify who is who.

Mr Joe Hegarty: My impression was that integration was slow. There weren't huge tensions, to say that would be to exaggerate things. On the whole, the Bangladeshis were a peaceful community and didn't give so many problems. Children tended to get to know each other in school and that was how it tended to happen, rather than through real adult integration.

Mr Hifzur Rahman: In the flat there were no neighbours, because the other rooms were offices. The only communication I had with people was when you go to the shops.

Getting involved in local issues

Ms Karen Buck MP: I remember being in Church Street for meetings with the Marylebone Bangladesh Society, which I think was then the only community organisation for Bangladeshis in Westminster, and it was huge! I used to come here with Mushtaq Qureshi, who sadly we've now lost, who was a councillor for a very long time.

We used to come for the Bangladeshi Independence Day celebrations, and it was brilliant. I remember going into the old North Westminster community school building in Church Street and we used to have 500 people in the room.

Mr Joe Hegarty: For a long time, it was a lot of big families, a very close knit community, but as time went on, people aspired to the same sort of values as other people, and gradually we've seen that happen with people moving on and moving out. We started to get councillors from the Bengali community and gain new community organisations. There were lots of things which were contributing factors to the area.

Mr Guthrie McKie: I think they have done. I'm very proud of our Bengali councillors – you see how they have mixed their role in their communities and their role as a councillor.

Having mixed friends

Haji Surok Meah: I did not allow them to play with other children, as in my area there were no Bengali children. Most of the Bengali families were on the other side, I mean in Lisson Green Estate. The behaviour of the children in Lisson Green was not very good. So my son always helped me at my restaurant, since he was 10.

Mr Hifzur Rahman: When I moved house, my child went to Gateway Nursery. There were a lot of Bengali kids. He kept contact with his best friend throughout primary school, but during secondary school his best friend passed away. He had other Bengali friends who he still kept in contact with; they see each other during different functions and events. I don't know if any of my children had any English friends.

Haji Fazar Ali: I had no fear. I was very happy they were socialising with different children.

Mrs Hosne Ara Moobin: My children played mostly with white children. There were very few Bengali children, one or two in one class.

Haji Arob Ali: No, actually they never attempted to mix with white children outside school, they did not have the chance to meet up with them, they only mixed within the school environment. I thought that they have to study with them and mix with them. Otherwise, how will they manage to be educated? I realised that they will not be able to do anything alone, living in isolation.

Alhaj Lala Miah: It was a mixed group. Like now, they have friends from different backgrounds. No, I allowed them to mix freely. I never stopped them mixing with their peer groups, but I always checked on them in the school and took care of their education. I always met their teachers and liaised with them, so that my children would have good grades.

As I did not hesitate to mix with the multicultural society, why would I prevent my children from mixing with others? I never thought that my children will be destroyed if they mixed with children of different cultures.

Mr Abdul Moobin: They mixed with their classmates and various children. I never advised them on what type of children they should play with; as long as they behaved well, it should be fine.

Haji Fazar Ali: They would play with a mixed group of children, like Bengali, Jamaican and English. In Gateway School there was a lot of Bengali.

Ms Khaleda Qureshi: They interacted mostly with English people, not many Bengalis were here so it was easy for them to divert towards the English culture. It was a big headache for us that there was no religious teacher available, how we can teach them about our religion?

Ms Syeda Chowdhury: It was mainly with white children in the school.

Mixed marriages

Alhaj Md Abdun Noor: Of course, I would not allow them to marry someone outside of my culture, not even of another faith. But the situation is different now, it is not possible to stop them.

Alhaj Lala Miah: I will accept it, as the situation has changed. This is not our time, this is their time, and they must make their own decisions.

Mr Abdul Hannan: I would not allow it at all.

Mrs Husna Ara Moobin: I never realised that my child would marry someone outside of my culture.
 In the beginning I had strong feelings about it, but now I realise that if they go for another culture or faith, what could I do about it?

Ms Khaleda Qureshi: I never gave this much thought, but we were always ready for it, as anything can happen.

Mr Hifzur Rahman: I am very open with my children. If they want to speak to me about anything, we speak freely.
 My child asked me 'If I like someone from another culture and I want to get married, what would be your answer?' I replied, 'Can you go into more detail, because this is something I would need to know a bit more about.' My child said, if they convert to become a Muslim, would you be ok with this?
 I told her, it depends on how much you feel for this person, but if your feelings are deep enough then I cannot say no. But then you will lose touch with me gradually. I tried to explain that I am not accepting this, but I was trying to explain it nicely. I gave various reasons: if your mother and I go to his house, we won't find a prayer mat.
 I would find it uncomfortable to eat in his house. His parents would feel the same in my house. So, the situation would not be nice. The relationships I have with the

families of the partners of my other two children won't be the same as with his family.

Sometimes they would attend white friend's birthday parties for 30 minutes. My daughter wanted to stay over at her friend's birthday party. I said she's not allowed to stay over, but she can go and visit and give a birthday gift.

When I first came I never understood Westminster Council. After I got the St John's Wood flat, I met someone who told me to come to meetings. I came one day and got put into the community. Now, I am very involved.

My children are highly religious. We celebrate birthdays just with cake. We don't celebrate Christmas, but we eat good food on Christmas day. My children are British but they are not entirely involved with the British culture. They are more involved with the Bengali culture.

Alhaj Muhib Uddin: He went to Gateway Primary School and his first friend was a white boy, as there were only one or two Bengalis.

There was no Bengali teacher, so after much thought the Bengali community formed the Marylebone Bangladesh Society, to create a Bengali culture for our children to be aware of and to not forget the Bengali culture.

Ms Azizun Khatun: Of course I have objections. All parents wish for their child to remain within their own culture. However, if anything different did happen, then I think we have to be positive.

Haji Arob Ali: We always nurtured our children into being Bengali, and to not adopt any other culture, and keep them away from other bad Bengali children. We always expected that our children should marry according to our tradition. We arranged that for them.

Mr Fazal Miah: They did not ask to do this, but had they asked, what could I do? Am I able to do much?

Mr Abdul Moobin: I never realised that my child would marry someone outside of my culture. I was a little worried that it would happen to them, but we never discouraged them from anything. We tried to teach them about our religion and tried to educate them about our Muslim culture.

It is natural, even though we taught them about our faith. Instead of that, they have been mixing with people of other faiths, so I don't know how I could have stopped them. But we tried to prevent them.

Chapter fourteen

Life in Westminster at present

Westminster has seen many changes over the years, and is generally described as more developed, with a stronger infrastructure and a denser population. However, some note that families have been priced out of the area, and it is now seen as a wealthy area.

The communities have also changed; some Bengalis remain but the Irish and Afro-Caribbean communities are mostly not around anymore, while a large Arab community has moved in. Bengalis also have less of a presence in local jobs.

However, there is now more diversity in the area and cultural festivals like Eid are now celebrated by a larger population.

Nonetheless, a sense of community has also been lost - many consider the new generation to treat each other with less respect than before, citing attitudes on buses as a prime example, where passengers have not given up seats for the elderly, or where bus drivers seem not to care for their passengers.

Alhaj Muhib Uddin: The change is like day and night. It is so much more developed now in Westminster, the buildings are better. The people are different; before the people were more English, now in Westminster it is more multicultural, more Arabic and Asian people. However, in Westminster it is harder for poor people to live here, as now there are many wealthier people.

Alhaj Abdur Rahman: Big differences in Westminster. During that time there were no big buildings like now, Marylebone flyover was built later on. This area looked very poor. Most of the area has been built up with high rise buildings after 1970, even Lisson Green was built in 1970, and this estate (Lisson Green) was the parcel depot of British Railway.

Ms Azizun Khatun: Lots of cultural changes have taken place in Westminster. Even in employment, I rarely saw someone from our community, but now there is a big change.

Mr Abdul Moobin: Not all of my life I was in Westminster, but I see that there are lots of changes in terms of housing and transport, and many other things have been developed.

Haji Arob Ali: Now more facilities are available than before. Previously there were no families here so only a couple of people celebrated Eid, but currently families are here so Eid enjoyment is completely different.

Alhaj Lala Miah: There are lots of changes in Westminster, for instance, the roads and streets have changed, new buildings have been built, more people are being educated, schools and colleges are increasing, people's standard of life has changed and massively improved.

Mrs Hosne Ara Moobin: Enormous changes. Density has been increased drastically. It's not the same in the shops, if you wish to buy anything you have to line up for a long period of time. More significantly, the change of attitude of bus drivers. During that time drivers were so polite and caring, whenever they would see a problem with a passenger, they would personally help. Everyone had respect for the elderly people.

Nowadays, people from different cultures and backgrounds have emerged in society, and sometimes I even see them taking elderly people's seats and not offering them to a needy person. It seems that the respect and the caring attitude of people has disappeared from society.

Mr Kobir Miah: To be honest, I don't know how Westminster functioned back then, but what I can say is today it is functioning well. I keep up to date with what Is happening within the community.

Alhaj Uster Ali: The community was strong. Now there is less respect amongst people. When people used to come over we used to help each other out with money. Everyone used to give, for example, a pound.

Ms Khaleda Qureshi: Lots of differences can be identified in term of people's behaviour. When I first came to this country I saw a lot of love and affection as well as good relationships amongst people, but nowadays those things seem to have disappeared. We can't blame others for this change, we are all responsible.

Ms Syeda Chowdhury: Now it's more like family. When we go to work now, all ethnicities are like one big family together. In April, I retired and left my full time job. The teachers that came from Australia said to me it felt like we lost our mum. They really cared for me and looked after me.

Ms Karen Buck MP: Some of the Bangladeshi community who bought flats, sometimes former council flats but not always, they couldn't be buying here anymore because it's too expensive. You've seen people go, some of the people who had a bit more money to make those choices. If it was a choice between a property of £500k and one of £200k, people will go for the cheaper.

When I first came to Westminster, it had a Bangladeshi community, particularly in Church Street, but also a very big Irish community, and a big Afro-Caribbean community, and now the Irish and Afro-Caribbean communities aren't really there anymore. They've moved on, as have some of the Bangladeshi community, and now we have an Arab community. 20 years on it will be different again, so movement and change is always part of the story.

Mr Guthrie McKie: We're now seeing young Bengalis have no trouble going into a pub. They may not have any alcohol, maybe just an orange juice and have a chat with people, so that's changed. And of course they speak English, as well as if not better than some of the white population.

I think that's the change, but there are still cultural ties with parents which make it difficult for some younger people. People, from all communities, often confuse culture and religion. They say 'that's my religion' when it's their culture – this thing about veils is a cultural thing.

The religion says nothing about that. It's about trying to have that dialogue – with the older generation they often say 'Well, that's my religion', when it isn't really.

Chapter fifteen

The British / Bangladeshi

Many parents are particularly happy with their children because they are practicing Muslims - religion is often considered the most important success criteria, and elicits the strongest opinions. Culture is less of a priority and brings out more mixed attitudes.

There is a general pride in viewing their children as equally Bengali and British. Parents are especially positive about education and financial security; they appreciate that their children have had to integrate with an English lifestyle in order to progress in their careers, and take pride in these successes.

There are, however, fears about what will happen with the next generation, caused by uncertainty about how those children will be raised.

Alhaj Md Abdun Noor: Perhaps their future may be the fattest? As a result of the English lifestyle, not ours. They are not bothered with their culture or religion.

Mr Khalil Miah: I'm very happy with my children. Both my sons were married in Bangladesh and still today they ask how I am.

Alhaj Md Abdun Noor: I was completely against the idea of bringing my children to this country, but later on, because of pressure from others, I decided to bring them here. But still I believe that I made a mistake, that I made the wrong decision. It would have been better if I hadn't brought them.

Alhaj Lala Miah: We changed our passports to British, but our children, to me, are 100% British. Our way of life and the British way of life are as different as day and night. In the same way that we have good connections with our own friends and family back home, similarly, in this country, they have their friends and community connections.

My eldest son is an HSBC consultant. He was in Bahrain and covered all of South Asia and toured most part of Bangladesh - Dhaka, Chittagong and Sylhet. After five years, this year he returned and told me that to him, Bangladesh is one of the richest countries in the world.

He said that if he had studied in Bangladesh, he could have become a minister, but he was raised in a western country, had studied here, and therefore is not able to understand everything. However, he has good connections with Bengalis.

Mr Abdul Hannan: They are Bengali and speak to me in Bengali always. They go to the mosque, pray and fast, which is enough. I am hopeful for their future. I am just very disappointed that my children will never go to Bangladesh. In Bangladesh nowadays, things are not as good as they used to be, it has deteriorated, so they will never be able to see my home. I have also not been able to educate them in what I would like them to learn. My wife wanted them to learn religion first. I am still happy, as they are good human beings.

Haji Fazar Ali: Yes, I am happy with them as they have turned out the way I expected. They have good links with the Bengali community but they also have their British culture. They make money and have British friends. They speak to me in Bengali and are good at communicating with the Bengali community.

Haji Surok Meah: I am happy to say that my children did very well. My daughter went to private school. I arranged a taxi for her every day to take her to school. I was financially very well off, as I did not have any other commitments back home. I still remember that I paid £2400 per quarter for her school fees. Now I am very happy for my children.

Ms Khaleda Qureshi: In terms of religious practice we never persuaded them, neither me nor my husband. Sometimes I asked my husband to get an Islamic teacher for them, but at that time it was really tough to get someone. But we tried to teach them as much as we know and they are doing namaaz and Ramadan.

Mr Hifzur Rahman: My eldest child got a degree. My youngest child did her A levels and now she's got a good job. Outside of education, I am very happy. I wanted them to socialise with others, and my children are good with socialising. They keep in contact with each other and still stay in contact with their family in Bangladesh.

Alhaj Lala Miah: I feel proud that my children had free access to the cosmopolitan society, therefore they were properly educated and are competing in the job market.

Ms Azizun Khatun: They feel they are fully British. At least in this generation they follow some of our culture, but as for the next generation, I don't know. They are believers, but not much practicing. I am very happy with their attainment.

Mr Abdul Sobur: My son continued to study here and went to secondary school here too, until it was time for him to move on to college, when he said to me that he can continue his studies here and get the qualifications to go to university from this school.

Then I said, that's fine, you can stay here, and stay with a school you are familiar with. Then he finished his studies here and passed, and went onto university and studied at Queen Mary University. He studied for three years there and then achieved his degree.

Mrs Hosne Ara Moobin: I still think they are Bengali, but they have been brought up in this country so they are British as well. They have strong connections with the Bengali community. They do Eid prayer or occasional religious activities, but I'm still struggling to get them to be regular practicing Muslims.

Both of my children did very well in their education

and also in their employment, praise to Allah, but the only area they need to improve on is their religious practice. I am still advising them to be religious and to keep the legacy of our faith and culture, asking them to at least carry on after our departure. Otherwise I am happy with them.

Alhaj Muhib Uddin: They have become more of a success than I ever expected, and all on their own, without asking me for any support, which I am very proud of. I love my children's British friends and always show them love. I do not mind how British my kids are because they do not forget their religion. They fast in Ramadan and give Zakat (charity) to the poor.

Mr Abdul Moobin: Yes, they fulfil my expectations and I am very happy. They are living like British people, they have been working in British society. I think 40% Bengali and 60% British.

How religious are they?

This is their choice, I never discourage or encourage them.

Mr Kobir Miah: Yes, 100%, they are 100% British. They are Bengali but they are also British. Yes, they are religious, they pray five times a day.

Mr Fazal Miah: What can I say, as they have got British passports, they are British. They are Bengali as well. Both of my children are practicing Muslims.

Ms Noorjahan Begum: I had a dream to educate my children but I could not, as they were not enthusiastic in education, but the current generation are doing their degrees or getting a good education. Only my youngest daughter did well, and has got a good job.

Ms Karen Buck MP: When I first knew the Bangladeshi community in the early 80s, they were not doing well educationally. These were new arrivals and their children were new arrivals, and often didn't have much education in Bangladesh either.

So that was a real battle that had to be fought, and I think that's been a remarkable success story. Now we see young Bengali people of the last 10 years doing really well educationally, and some of the most improved results of any community in Britain, which is extraordinary and very good.

Well, I think education is a success story, and education itself will break down some of those barriers. I go to some of the award ceremonies, and they're handing out awards for extraordinary results at school, and those young people have got prospects now that they didn't have before, to go into professions and business and just do very well.

The other thing that I think is really good is that we now have significant Bengali political representation, including in Parliament. We still have more to do but at local authority level we've had a Mayor. I don't agree with the politics but it's still really important that we have political representation within each of the communities, and it should be more than one party.

Chapter sixteen

Future hopes

The Bengali community mostly longs for their children to remain religious and for prosperity in their careers. They also want future generations to have the same.

Alhaj Lala Miah: They do namaaz and Ramadan but at this age how much more can you expect? They give Zakat and follow the sunnah of the Prophet. In some cases they are better than us.

The future of our community is very bright, as many of our children are becoming doctors, engineers, barristers and solicitors etc. They have been occupying various employment positions. I am sure they will go far.

I am happy and feel proud. At least, we should be proud that our generation has been happy, having a good life.

Mr Hifzur Rahman: Everything I taught my children, they will teach their children.

Alhaj Muhib Uddin: All I want is that all my children pray five times, and that would be enough for me.

Mr Kobir Miah: Honestly, when I think about the future, these days it's very hard. However, God knows. I want my children to prosper, work hard and live well.

Chapter seventeen

Bangladeshis in the eyes of others

The Bangladeshi community appears to be progressing well; education has generally been strong and the successes are paying off with many people working in many different fields. However, this is not always the case, and many people continue to work in the same careers as their parents. They encourage education for the Bangladeshi community and sympathise with housing and employment concerns.

Mr Mohammed Siraj: A major change which I have noticed is that the youngsters who have grown up can speak English. The communication has changed. The parents can communicate through the children now, which is better, and the outlook has changed as well now.

The kids have starting doing well now. I've noticed that. Before, the parents were not interested in study. They wanted them to join the business. But now I see they're progressing in different fields, which is for the better of the community.

Ms Karen Buck MP: I think the Bangladeshi community has a great deal to be proud of. They are an extremely hard working community and I think they've come along in leaps and bounds in terms of educational achievement for their children, and I think that's brilliant and it is overwhelmingly a successful migration story.

But we have to remember that several things can be true at the same time, and one of the things that is true is that there's still quite a lot of disadvantage, including housing and employment. The story is never finished.

Mr Guthrie McKie: I think it's headed for great change. I mean, I see it in people like you. I see people aged 18, 20, 22, on a career path that would be completely alien to their parents. Their parents must be very proud of them – they wouldn't understand the world that that takes them into.

Being skilled and succeeding in a career changes you as an individual, it opens your eyes and it widens your perspective of the world.

Mr Mohammed Siraj: I think they are progressing. Kids especially are doing well but some of them obviously have gone the wrong way, but that can't be helped. But the majority from what I see have done very well, and I think that's good for the community.

One thing I really appreciate is that Bengalis have always supported me right through, and vice versa. I have tried to help them whenever and wherever I could. What I would like to see improved is the mentality of children; I know most of them are going to university but there are children who do not want to do that, and I don't understand why.

They need drumming in to them that education is the main thing. Still, there are certain parents who want their son to go into the restaurant business or somewhere like that; they should just try to change that, it will be better. And the answer I think lies with the fathers; whenever they get together in the community centres, like when you have a function or anything, they should really drum it into them that education is the future.

Chapter eighteen

Views of our community researchers

Afzal Rahman
Community researcher and editorial team

As the children and grandchildren of immigrants, we grow up hearing stories from older generations about leaving home and settling into a new country. These stories of migration are often filled with hardship, but the powerful forces behind them are those of hope and aspiration.

Bangladeshi migrants who moved to London in the 70s came with very little, but they spent their lives laying the foundations on which our generation builds. Many of us inherited their sense of purpose, and it can be difficult to find the time to stop and take stock of what got us to where we are.

With this in mind we brought together a group of young volunteers to begin a conversation within our community, to reflect, and to record these memories before they are lost. The stories speak for themselves and we hope this book will inspire others to have similar conversations with their grandparents, parents, aunts and uncles.

Juned Mohammed Mehrajul Islam
Editorial team

The impact of the arrival of the first mass wave of Bengali migrants in the 60s and 70s is well documented. From the changing face of the East End of London to opening up their now world-famous restaurants, Bengalis have helped shape the idea that the UK is a multicultural country where different cultures can come together to succeed.

We often hear about the successes of these people, but what is not extensively recorded is first-hand accounts from the Bengalis themselves. The personal struggles of arriving in a new country, the professional discrimination, the racism and the overcoming of obstacles.

As a person of Bengali origin, I thought I understood the struggles of those before me. I wanted to document what I already knew, for people who were unaware. Working on this project has revealed a great deal that I never knew existed. It revealed stories of friendship, compassion, and acceptance. There is so much more that we still do not know, and now is the ideal time to find out.

Abu Sorwar Toki
Community research team / Technical lead

It has been an amazing opportunity for us to investigate the history of those that have made a life changing decision to relocate to Westminster. We often hear of the struggles in Bangladesh, and how the lives of many have been affected.

However, their lives in Westminster have never been explored and, from my perspective, that is equally beneficial for our knowledge. This is what inspired me to be involved in this project. This history was about my ancestors in the borough that I currently live in - to play a role in uncovering their tales has been a great learning opportunity for me.

It is difficult to pinpoint my favourite part of this project, as all aspects of it have been so beneficial for my learning. I have learnt to work as part of a team, to plan the investigation, to develop our hypothesis and then set out to investigate. We were well supported and trained to feel and act like true researchers.

This project has enabled me to get back in touch with my roots. I have been inspired to learn more about my heritage and the culture that my family come from.

This project has been thoroughly enjoyable for me. During the interviews (off camera), I really built a good relationship with the Bengali migrants, and enjoyed listening to their tales and jokes. Their difficult times have been inspirational for me. My favourite part would be hearing how the older generation used their free time; it was amusing to hear that that people like my granddad used to go to the cinema, I would never think in a million years that my granddad would enjoy going to the cinema.

I hope to see more projects such as this, that help young people explore and celebrate hidden parts of their culture, it has made me feel even more proud of my Bangladeshi heritage. I am very grateful to the organisers for helping me appreciate and get back in touch with my culture.

Mobena Ahmed
Community research team

The reason this project appealed to me is because of the importance of history. I completed a history A Level a few years ago and I found that it allows each and every one of us to acknowledge that cultural, ethnic and national identity is very significant, especially in today's society, where we have evolved into such great paths.

Hearing and learning about our hometowns, home countries, and related cultures has allowed me to gain a more meaningful insight into our ancestral roots, and how we got to where we are today.

This experience that I have been fortunate enough to be a part of has allowed me to embrace my identity, and be able to share countless stories with friends and family. It has allowed us to examine chains of events, and understand how one small occurrence can spark countless, invaluable incidents, and begin to understand the nature of change.

I hope in the future this book enables a trend through our following generations, where we can document our cultural diversity and experiences. I have faith this will encourage youngsters in my generation, and the generations after us, to inspire us to be the best we can be, due to the struggles our lineages have faced. Further, I anticipate it will encourage individuals to have the strength to pursue goals to develop a valuable perspective as we grapple with our problems, and try to prepare for a prosperous future.

Tahmina Ahmed
Community research team

I wanted to be involved in this project in order to gain further knowledge about the Bengali culture, and how the past has shaped Bengalis today.

This project was interesting because, as a British person with a Bengali background, it was not difficult growing up in this country, due to my family living here and not facing much discrimination against ethnic minorities. This contrasts sharply with the 1960s.

The fact that Bangladeshi migrants had to settle in Britain without most of their family, and in a population full of British-born people, it intrigued me so much that I wanted to interview them personally, in order to understand the struggles they had experienced when they first came to Britain. Furthermore, it was appealing to find out the various factors that played a part in motivating Bengalis to migrate to Britain.

I enjoyed taking part in this project as it was a privilege to communicate with individuals who had played a major role in the British Bengali culture, as they shared their inspiring life stories. It is not an opportunity you get every day, to find out about my own culture, so I felt very pleased to gain more insight into the Bengali culture.

Mr Azim Chowdhury
Community research team
I chose to get involved in this project as it gave me an opportunity to learn more about my dual heritage and contribute towards a special part of my history. Hearing the stories of those before me, has not only been exciting for me but also inspiring for me and my family. I have really learnt to value those closest to me, and feel more invested in their stories. Stories that I will continue to re-tell to the generations that follow.

Prior to this project, I had never been involved in any community related projects, so this was a great opportunity for me to meet some of the local people of Westminster, build new networks, and learn new skills. I think projects such as these, create wonderful opportunities for new generations to connect and share strengths. I would encourage more of my peers to contribute to our growing multicultural society by collecting and sharing stories of their heritage. History enables us to not only learn lessons for the future, but contribute to the building of a richer and more meaningful identity.

Tamirol Islam
Community research team

Faces of Westminster is a project which holds deep historical significance within the British Bangladeshi community, particularly with past and current residents of the borough. As a British Bangladeshi who resides in Westminster, this project resonated with me as it explored themes of culture, integration and community.

The significance of this project is profound, being that it accounts for the experiences of individuals who immigrated to the borough during the 70s and 80s, which otherwise may never have been documented. The oral accounts of the participants provide the readers with an authentic narrative of the social and economic triumphs made in establishing one's self during this period of time.

As a young British Bangladeshi, this project has been deeply insightful. It has allowed me to understand the significant contribution and sacrifices many individuals of my community have made, in order to establish a foundation for future generations.

Abu Taher Toki
Community research team

Growing up as a British Bangladeshi I was guilty of a lack of knowledge about the heritage which I come from. I knew many people within the Bangladeshi community, but had never heard about their own struggles and barriers. Countless times during the interviews, after hearing stories about how brave individuals sacrificed their families, friends and possessions, I was left dry mouthed and teary eyed.

The closest I could relate to these fearless men and women, was moving away to university. However, even then, I had the support of my family and I was only a train journey away from home. During my schooling years, I had learnt about numerous great individuals, but never did I fathom that there would be so many walking the streets of Westminster today.

As we dove deeper into this area, it became more apparent why this research was vital. The fact no one had ever created a project like this seemed absurd. The thought that after 20 years, many of these tales would have never been told, if not for this project, is ludicrous. It is essential for these stories to be read by many other people, not just young British Bangladeshis such as myself.

My favourite part of this project was the interview stage. On more than one occasion I forgot about my role as an interviewer, because I was lost in the stories. I came to realise that the best stories are not from fiction or films, but from the generations that came before us.

I found it very refreshing to hear about the support the Bangladeshi community received to help them with their integration into society.

Simply going to the doctors or pharmacist was a big hurdle, and without the support from individuals outside the community it would have definitely been a more daunting task. I have to admit that hearing some of the challenges the Bangladeshi community faced, has put some of my own barriers in perspective.

We should definitely conduct more projects like this in the future. It is important to explore under-researched areas, and bring to light stories of other cultures which are at risk of being lost. I am deeply grateful to CLYD for involving me in such an eye-opening and enriching project. I would also like to thank all the individuals who have shared their stories with me, because in order to know where I am going, it was important for me to know where I had come from.

Fahmida Rahman
Community research team

This project appealed to me because its cause was so central to my own heritage and history. The journeys that Bangladeshi migrants made in the 60s and 70s dramatically altered the trajectories of the generations that followed them. The struggles they faced and the sacrifices that they made laid the foundations for the many successes of the burgeoning British Bangladeshi community of today.

The importance of documenting this history was clear to me from the outset. Much of my own desire to work hard, not only to achieve my personal goals, but also to strive for a better future for my family and the community around us, derives from my understanding of the struggles and sacrifices of my parents and grandparents. However, as these people grow older and approach the end of their lives, true knowledge of their legacy was in danger of being lost forever. This project provided a platform to preserve this legacy for the continued benefit of future generations.

I thoroughly enjoyed taking part in this project, and the opportunity that it provided to interact with so many courageous and inspiring individuals. I also greatly benefitted from the opportunity to develop my research and interviewing skills, and to diversify my communication skills. As an aspiring academic I believe that these skills will be of great use in my future.

Tahmidur Rahman
Community research team

Our place in this country is defined by the generations above us, who put us here. Not only do we have our own responsibilities to define our own identities in 21st century Britain, but we also need to understand where these identities came from. The only way to do that is to talk to those who've lived those times, and to document their accounts before they're lost.

I believe it's fundamental that our histories are kept not simply for ourselves, but also for our children and theirs too, primarily because histories unveil truths about the present – ultimately, understanding past and present realities sets the ground from which we begin to campaign for the longevity and futures of our communities.

I was particularly interested in hearing individual stories; history is best recounted anecdotally when you're personally attached to the narratives. The opportunity to communicate with an older generation through their narratives sounded like an amazing way to bridge the generation gap, by working through their memories of an area we've grown up in.

Moreover, the promise of stories invites the personal asides, interesting little comments and individual characters into the histories.

This kind of research pierces straight through to the fact that these histories have rarely been documented.

The appropriate academic disciplines for the content have ignored this fundamental part of the creation of London, because this history is commonly not a part of the historian's background and they are, therefore, not tied to the narratives.

This means that if I were to look for an appropriate book on the topic, I wouldn't be able to find it, which means people need to write it, which ultimately means the initiative is on the descendants of the interviewed, or us. If we don't do it, nobody will, and then our history will be forgotten, as will a crucial element of our understanding of our lives in London today - the generations to come won't know what the people who brought them here wanted for them.

I most enjoyed reading through all of the stories and opinions and working my way through the information they'd given us. I loved to hear the perspectives they have on our lives because it's clearly something they care about, and something we need to take into account when looking at how we're going about our lives.

I'd love to see more research of this kind. Specific histories need to be documented and I hope that this topic gains some more interest. Hopefully, we've encouraged readers to get involved in this sort of work, we've at least begun to fill a gaping hole of knowledge and ultimately, hopefully, I'll be seeing more projects like this one (and even getting involved with them too).

Romena Toki
Community research team

As British Bangladeshis, whose grandparents moved to the UK in the 1960s and 1970s, this project was very close to our heart. We don't often get the chance to hear or share their stories. They are ageing, and we realised that it won't be long before their stories are lost to oblivion, which is why 'Faces of Westminster' has been launched.

Giving first generation Bengali migrants a voice is a key agenda of Faces of Westminster. It has been an absolute honour and privilege to document the stories of our British and Bengali heritage.

Faces of Westminster celebrates the good, highlights the bad, and hopefully inspires action in our youth. History is not just found in academic texts – history can be at home, locked in the memories of our loved ones.

Standing: Mehrajul, Tamirol, Aziz Toki, Tahmid, Afzal, Nisa
Seating : Romena, Fahmida & Sorwar

From left: Afzal, Mehrajul, Tamirul, Romena, Ansar Ahmed Ullah, Fahmida, Nisa,Tahmidul & Sorwar

Chapter nineteen

The first generation

Below are the Bangladeshi migrants who have kindly shared their incredible stories with us.

Alhaj Uster Ali

Mr Hifzur Rahman

Alhaj Muhib Uddin

Ms Azizun Khatun

Mr Kobir Miah

Mr Abdul Moobin

Ms Noorjahan Begum	Haji Arob Ali	Alhaj Lala Miah
Mrs Hosne Ara Moobin	Ms Syeda Chowdhury	Mr Abdul Sobur
Mr Fazal Miah	Haji Fazar Ali	Ms Khaleda Qureshi

Mr Abdul Hannan

Alhaj Abdur Rahman

Mrs Anowara Begum

Haji Surok Meah

Mr Alhaj Md Abdun Noor

Mrs Harisun Nessa

Mr Khalil Miah

Service providers and local community members and politicians

Hilda Griffith
A member of the community

Mr Mohammed Siraj
Pharmacist

Dr Andrew Elder
GP

Ms Karen Buck
MP

Mr Joe Hegarty
Community Leader

Cllr Guthrie McKie
Councillor